Couple Communication After a Baby Dies

DIFFERING PERSPECTIVES

by

Sherokee Ilse and Tim Nelson

A special thank you to our spouses, Monica and David, who let us tell our versions of our story and who still love us.

Sherokee, David, Monica, and Tim travelling in England before attending the 2007 International Stillbirth Alliance Conference in Birmingham, United Kingdom.

Thank you also to:

Sandra and Ryan Doherty, Julie Alnon, Pat Flynn of Missing Angels USA, Charmayne Hollis, Lori Martini, Alicia Nimmo of SIDS and KIDS, Marie Hagberg, Susan Erling Martinez, Calvin deRuyter of A Place To Remember

A Place To Remember, 1885 University Ave. West, Suite 110, St. Paul, MN 55104; 651-645-7045; FAX 651-645-4780; EMAIL tn@APlaceToRemember.com; www.APlaceToRemember.com

Wintergreen Press, Inc., 3630 Eileen Street, Maple Plain, MN 55359; 952-476-1303; EMAIL sherokeeilse@yahoo.com; www.wintergreenpress.com

ISBN 978-1-883525-03-3

Table of Contents

About the authors

Sherokee Ilse, a bereaved mother who has experienced a miscarriage (Marama), stillbirth (Brennan), and an ectopic pregnancy (Bryna), is also the mother of two healthy sons (Kellan and Trevor) and married for over 30 years to David. Motivated by her early losses, Sherokee wrote one of the first books on infant loss, *Empty Arms: Coping with Miscarriage, Stillbirth, and Infant Death....Surviving the First Hours and Beyond.* WIth over 300,000 copies in print, it was revised in 2008. Since her first loss, she has become an international speaker and trainer on this subject as well as on general bereavement. *Couple Communication* is Sherokee's seventeenth book/booklet on the subject of loss. She continues to stay actively involved in this issue working to improve the care of bereaved families and promote research in stillbirth and infant death. To learn more about her, or to reach her, visit her website — www.wintergreenpress.com.

Tim Nelson, and his wife Monica, experienced the full-term stillbirth of their second child, Kathleen. Following his daughter's death, Tim wrote, *A Father's Story - When a Baby Dies*, one of the first perinatal loss support booklets for men. He also volunteered with the Pregnancy and Infant Loss Center, eventually serving as president of the board of directors. In the mid-1990s, the communications and design business he co-owns founded A Place To Remember, a company that publishes and distributes resources worldwide for grieving families and their caregivers. In 2004, he authored *A Guide For Fathers - When A Baby Dies,* a pocket-sized resource for bereaved dads. He is also the publisher of *Born to Fly – An Infant's Journey to God.* Tim is certified by the Grief Recovery® Institute as a training specialist, and conducts outreach programs for those experiencing change and loss in their lives. He has spoken both nationally and internationally on topics of grief and loss, specifically as they relate to men. He has four living children.

Introduction

You may have chuckled to yourself when you noticed that this book focuses on couple communication, yet, it is not written by a couple. This is no coincidence. It speaks loudly to what many people find to be true...after a traumatic event, it is often easier to talk about your fears and feelings with people other than your partner.

We, David and Sherokee and Tim and Monica, have been good friends for more than 20 years. Our babies' deaths brought us together. Our friendship grew over time, in part, because of the strength we found from having another couple to share our ups and downs. Sometimes the simple knowledge that we weren't the only couple to struggle after our babies' death gave us the courage to keep working on our relationships. It was also easier to laugh at ourselves as individuals when we knew our interactions and miscommunications as married couples were not unique. And it was somehow less threatening to hear a friend of the opposite sex talk about their feelings than it was our mate.

That is why we, Sherokee and Tim, decided to put this book together. Not every couple has others to talk with like we did (and spouses who supported us in this endeavor.) We hope that by sharing our intimate journeys—journeys that have the benefit of hindsight—you will find something useful as you and your partner work through this challenging time.

While the four of us discovered our reactions to certain issues and concerns were often divided along gender lines, this was not consistent, and we were by no means clones of one another. We also noticed that some issues were difficult for one couple but not necessarily for the other. We also realized that while differences in coping styles came up in our relationships, what kept us together was our shared love for our baby. We each were hurt deeply and were changed profoundly because of this little one we had created together. Remembering that which bound us to each other, helped us cope with our daily ups and downs.

This book is not really about us; it is about each of you and how YOU are coping. Our stories and suggestions are meant to fuel conversation in YOUR relationship. You may find that one of you is more intuitive, expressing grief in an affective/emotional way (like Sherokee and Monica) and the other in a more introspective or logical manner where grief is often expressed actively/physically but not necessarily verbally (like Tim and David.) While this can follow along gender lines, clearly it is not always so. Whatever the case, remember to seek out what you have in common and what binds you to each other. You both have been crushed by this loss and you both love this baby.

We certainly understand that you bring your own set of circumstances, both as individuals and as a couple, to this traumatic event. You may agree, or disagree, with what we have to say. Or, you may not want to hear what is being said. (David suggested you might even be angry with some of what we suggest.) Everyone is different.

If you are reading this book, we assume you have concluded that making your relationship stronger is a worthy goal — one that will require work, communication, understanding, and most of all, patience.

The book's structure

- We begin with some of our thoughts on issues that many couples face as they grieve the loss of their child, whether from miscarriage, stillbirth, SIDS, or early infant death;
- Next, we each look back on our lives at the time of our losses and share our stories. In some cases, we include other people's thoughts as they relate to relationships with their partners. We discuss not only what we have learned in the years following our loss, but also how we felt as a woman and a man facing those obstacles at the time, sharing thoughts and advice;
- We end sections by offering suggestions for couples to consider as they face similar challenges;

- After we share our stories, we present more thoughts from other couples on some of the topics we touched on throughout the book;
- Near the end of the book, we offer a place for you to take notes and reflect. There are also some questions to encourage conversation between you and your partner. Hopefully, the questions will stimulate more thoughts and questions of your own. You may then use what you have written as a starting point for discussion in the privacy of your own home, in a counseling setting, or within a support group;
- A few resources are shared at the end.

Some things to think about...

No matter what stage in pregnancy, or how old your baby was at the time of his/her death, you are a parent who has suffered the ultimate tragedy. Our hearts go out to you. There are some universal issues that many couples face at a time like this, so please know you are not alone if you find yourselves struggling.

As a couple you may have many feelings and fears: "Will we make it?" "Do we want to?" "What do we do now?" "S/he doesn't understand!" "Can I help my spouse get through this?" "How do I help my spouse?" You may feel like the bottom has dropped out, yet you are expected to go on—for your partner, possibly for your other children, or for someone else. You may wonder if you can.

We have been there. We have known pain and sorrow and have struggled to keep going, even during the times we did not think we would make it.

This crisis can shake the very core of your relationship, changing each of you forever. Having lived it, we can honestly say this is a long process of healing which begins with deep hurting. But we can also testify to the fact that it is not only possible to heal from this experience, it is also within your reach to grow both as individuals and as a couple. If you are recently married, you may find the challenges of your new relationship complicated further by this tragic event. But no matter how long you have been together, keeping your love for each other in mind will be critical.

Love and loss are a part of life, just as joy and sorrow are part of the human experience. Don't add to your pain by attempting to deny your loss, but instead work toward accepting it. It has happened, and now you must live through it as you pave the road to healing and renewal.

Seeking hope and 'rainbows' following a storm can help you. As you cultivate your coping skills and learn to survive and grow, you will also likely gain confidence that will benefit you in the future. Certainly, we know you would not have chosen to grow in this way, but it is okay to embrace the lessons you are learning.

What we have written in the following section addresses some things to consider as you make your way through this book and work on your relationship. We want you to know as much as you can about our thoughts and what this book is based upon before we begin sharing our stories

A challenge to our faith

A tragedy like this often triggers an immediate examination of one's faith. You may ask how and why do such horrible things happen to good people? Who would allow this kind of pain? Whether you have a strong faith in God, or a sense of spirituality that guides you, this incident can shake you to the very depths of your being. Questioning one's personal beliefs can happen even to the most faithful.

Communication is a two-way street... (with lots of potholes)

Communication is not only what you say, but how it is perceived by the person listening. Communication is also what you don't say as you interact.

Judging each other's words and deeds by using your intuition, or making guesses, is dangerous in both the short and long term of a relationship. When you are in doubt, don't assume, instead check it out—ask. Often couples find themselves misinterpreting looks given and words spoken. Remember that you are seeing your partner through your own pain. Understanding others is a tricky business on ordinary days; it is even more confusing and difficult when the fog of grief surrounds you on that winding street full of potholes.

When you are both feeling relaxed, take the time and risk to ask your partner how s/he is feeling. Don't pick highly intense and emotional moments, because the likelihood of the conversation escalating into an argument increases dramatically. By raising the question at a calm time, you show a genuine interest in what your partner is thinking and show compassion and understanding for his or her perspective.

Making communication a priority, even during difficult times, could be the key to saving your marriage and strengthening your love for each other.

The roles of men and women

It seems that throughout the ages the role of women during a crisis, such as death, has remained relatively consistent. Women often comfort each other through physical means— hugs and close presence. They bring each other food, and they usually talk about what has happened. This has not changed for generations. What has changed, however, is the role of men during these times. In the past, men were expected to do something while the women comforted each other. Men would often make the burial casket, dig the grave, and deal with the physical things associated with death. Now funeral homes and cemetery workers take care of those tasks. One of the most difficult positions in a crisis situation is to be the one who has nothing to do. This lack of an active role can further complicate a grieving father's place. Because many men have a need to be physically active as they process their feelings, give this issue some thought as you make your plans; be both creative and understanding of its importance.

Personality and past experiences often influence how each of us grieves

While this concept seems simple, taking the time to understand it has the potential to make a significant difference in how you understand and cope with each other's attitudes and behaviors.

The basis for how you grieve is influenced by your personality, life experiences, view of male/female roles, family dynamics, and more. People tend to grieve relative to their beliefs and past experiences since that is the basis of their comfort zone. And while there may be strong reasons to challenge some of those beliefs and perceptions, it is not realistic to expect dramatic change to come during the most raw and early times. As one care provider pointed out, "If someone is drowning, most likely that is not the best time to try and teach them a new swimming stroke."

If you understand the influence personal history and personality have on behavior, you might be more open to allow the differences between you, your partner, and even your relatives and friends. It might also be easier to discover the type of people you need to surround yourself with and to forgive people who offer up unhelpful or even hurtful advice. For instance, some people are 'buck up' types who want to move on rather than dwell on things. Others see the positive (or negative) in everything, while others are either introverted or extroverted. There are people who keep everything to themselves or live in a logical and rational manner. And there are those who wear everything on their sleeves, needing to vent and share their feelings. Thinking about your partner's and your own personality style can help you communicate better.

It is also helpful to give some thought to how differently men and women have been socialized. From early on, many boys are taught to be brave, take charge, be in control, not cry, and be the 'man of the house.' What is implied in all these life lessons is that men are responsible for taking care of their family and protecting them from harm. When a child dies, the very foundation of what a man has been taught all his life is challenged, resulting in an even greater need for him to try and concentrate on tasks he can control. Meanwhile, girls are taught to prepare for motherhood and run a household, as well as balance all those responsibilities with a career. Emotions are necessary and normal to share; crying and venting are acceptable. For women, there seems to be permission to stay focused on emotions and the journey rather than moving on too quickly...staying mad or upset even for days and days. Some women may be quiet and calm, while others may be more open and expressive.

Both individual personality and life experiences make you who you are. Explore that as you relate to each other throughout this time.

How does the death of a child affect a couple's relationship?

Be aware that you are likely to hear from well-meaning friends, family, or even some counselors, that many marriages will break up following the loss of a child. We have yet to see any credible studies proving this statement to be true, nor have we met or heard from many couples who broke up. We fear it can be a self-fulfilling prophecy if couples hear it too often. There is little doubt that the divorce rate may be high, but there is no reason that we are aware of which puts you at greater risk now than you were prior to your loss.

Will you have struggles? Yes, it is true that you may both be fragile for a long time and there will be shaky times. You will need to seek out your new 'normal,' since this experience does change each of you forever.

If your marriage was fairly strong going into this experience, you have an advantage and some familiarity with each other to fall back upon. If you feel your relationship was not that strong before this crisis or that you are still learning how to cope together under adversity, you may want to seek support and counseling early on. Why wait until cracks develop or grow deeper? Get help early in order to work through the difficult times ahead. In any case, you may well find yourselves closer than ever during and/or after some of the shock wears off. Most of the couples we hear from have found this to be so. Yet, there are those couples who have split up, probably due at least in part to previous on-going problems, struggles and coping styles. A devastating experience such as this can add to the rift, making the the divide too wide to heal. You both are still good people, and if you wish for your relationship to survive, maybe the thoughts contained in this book can be of help.

Getting through this requires good communication for your diverse coping styles and healing needs and for the reminder of your love for each other. It is possible to weather this together, survive, and thrive as a couple.

Give each other the benefit of the doubt

Believe the best, rather than the worst. This simple thought can make a world of difference in daily communication. Instead of thinking a certain comment or look was meant to be criticism, believe it was meant as a compliment or something positive. Assume you each have the best intentions. Instead of turning something into a disagreement, it can become a pleasant moment, or at least not the beginning of an argument. Try not to project any anger you feel onto your partner.

Decisions made early on often become the foundation for future interactions in your relationship

All any of us can do when living through a crisis is to try to make the best decisions possible. But there are some relatively common pitfalls that can be avoided. Be aware that if one person makes decisions for a partner without consulting her/him, it can be a source of conflict down the road. For example, some individuals have expressed regret about the amount of time they spent with their baby after death because their partner decided it was best to hurry that time along. Some individuals believed it was wise or helpful to go to a support group or counseling while their partner did not want to go. Keep in mind that when one person pressures their partner to make a decision against their wishes, rather than seeking a compromise, they are opening themselves to becoming a target of blame later on.

Just because it looks broken to you, does not mean it needs fixing

We all know people who have a strong need to offer solutions to other's problems. When a death occurs, this 'fix-it' type immediately begins searching high and low for the right tools to make it better. If they find that one tool does not work, they frantically search for another. In addition, the one to be 'fixed' might often look to their partner to fix things for them and can be very disappointed when they realize their partner cannot make them all better.

While a 'fixer' can certainly be either a man or a woman, it does seem that dads frequently take on this role after the death of a child. Possibly because men are raised to believe they need to be protectors of their family, they find it difficult to just sit with their partner in a puddle of tears, replaying the injustice and anguish of this tragedy. Often, it seems, men are propelled by a sense of responsibility to take some sort of action—to do something. Undoubtedly, there are many times in a couple's life where this is a highly valued attribute—when the tire goes flat, a sound or smell awakens you in the night, or there is a threat to life or home. However, after a bay dies, there is nothing anyone can do to fix it or make it significantly better. Unfortunately, some individuals do not come to this realization until they are well into the grieving process and have learned the hard way that their good intentions are not useful or even wanted.

Other people look to their support system, particularly their mate, to stand by them while they dwell, replay, and remember the baby and the full details of the experience. They simply want to live the moment, even when it is painful, and have no desire to take any kind of action. In their own way, they need to *be* in the experience. And while they may openly share their sadness and frustrations aloud, they are not really looking to be fixed or given advice about how to move forward. They simply feel better if they vent, getting it off their chest.

Brain differences may influence how we grieve

No, we don't mean one of you is brighter than the other. However, there are some recent studies ("The Female Brain", 2006, Louann Brizendine, and Dr. Godfrey Pearlson at Hopkins University) that examine the brain differences in how most men and women are wired. Though there will always be exceptions in studying large populations, some of these differences are reported as generalizations. This study suggests that many women excel at knowing what people are feeling, while many men may have difficulty spotting emotion unless someone cries, threatens bodily harm, or it is made very clear to them. Therefore, some women may appear to be overly sensitive to situations and what their partner says, does, or does not do. On the other hand, many men may not see or understand when emotional signals are being sent, and would possibly benefit from directness. This might explain why some bereaved mothers are easily upset by the words and behaviors of others that go unnoticed by the fathers. And it may also explain why some men do not easily pick up on women's moods or needs. Along these lines, it seems that women are more likely to remember fights or events that a man insists never happened — further complicating the process of getting along.

Research also indicates that many women are more naturally verbal than men. In fact, one study suggests that women speak 20,000 words on average each day, while men speak 7,000 (could that be why Sherokee's sections of this book are longer and more verbose?). Given that most women seem to rely more on language to cope with daily life (and to vent during frustrating or painful times) than men do, it makes sense that the differences in communication are real. While women sometimes expect men to speak more about their loss, that may be unrealistic and unfair. On the other hand, men might wish that their partners speak less about the baby and their daily grieving experiences, which is equally unrealistic and unfair.

In another study (S.E. Taylor, UCLA, 2002), women appear to respond to stress with a cascade of brain chemicals that cause them to 'tend children and gather with others.' This making and maintaining of friendships with other women is called the *tend/befriend tendency*. The oxytocin, which is released in the brain during these nurturing and befriending times, calms women, thus motivating them to reach out to others to share their pain. Meanwhile, plenty of studies show that men's testosterone levels increase under stress, resulting in either a fight or flight mode. Therefore, their need to 'do' something or 'escape' makes sense.

Even when things are going well, most women find friends to talk with when needed. However, a natural tendency when a baby dies is to expect your partner to be the one to give support. It may even feel like a betrayal to need others. Yet, apparently, it is very important for women to seek out others to befriend while sharing emotions and traveling the grief journey.

Just knowing that there could be a difference in brain patterns may help you understand your partner better and maybe help you forgive him or her for doing things differently than you wish. Honor each other not only in how you cope together, but also in how you are different.

However, none of this is meant to be a reason to let each other off the hook or to not take steps toward communicating.

What could this mean for you as a couple?

Women:

- Don't beat around the bush and hope he notices. Instead, speak up and tell him what you feel and what you want or expect from him. There is no point in resenting him because you think he doesn't care or isn't paying attention.

- Forgive him if he cannot honor every request. And console and support him when you are able;

- Don't expect your partner to be your main support person. But if he is, and it is working for you, be grateful for this gift that is not common for all couples;

- You may wish to seek out other women, particularly those who have been through something similar, since you may need to dwell on this and retell the story;

- Try not to be overly sensitive to everything he says, does, or does not do;

- If he attempts to fix you, which is out of his love and protectiveness, gently suggest that is not helpful right now and give him ideas on what *is* helpful;

- He may not be able to just *be* with you very often. Instead, encourage him to take action where he can, which honors his need to *do* something productive;

- If you find yourself dwelling on the sorrow too long or cannot find enough support, it may be time to seek counseling or other support.

Men:

- When you are feeling fearful and like life is out of control, take time to tell her your feelings. She has them, too. Knowing you are both vulnerable at times can be a bond between you and doesn't leave her wondering what you are thinking or if you really still care;

- Watch for signs that she may be upset, but also tell her that you want her to be open with you, so you don't have to play the guessing game;

- You may need to let her talk even when you don't feel like listening;

- Fight the urge to offer solutions. What she needs is someone who will just listen and hold her. Be that as often as you can;

- Encourage her to find other women she can befriend for added support;

- Stoicism, silence, and grieving in your head may feel right for you, but this keeps your partner out of your process. Make the effort to share your feelings sometimes;

- If you have the need to *do* something special, search for meaningful ways, and let your partner know why it is important to you;

- If you feel the need to escape, tell her what you are doing and why, so she doesn't think you don't love her or are escaping from *her*;

- If you are preoccupied or escaping often, ask yourself, your partner, or even a counselor to help determine if it is too much.

Living through the death of your baby

Our stories and our 'couple communication' at the time

Sherokee After five years of marriage, David and I felt it was time to work on having a baby. When we found ourselves pregnant, then suddenly miscarrying, it was quite a shock for which we were unprepared. In my mind after a few years, I named that baby Marama, and we agreed to disagree that it was a girl (my feeling but not his.) We didn't do very well in our communication or healing at that time. Instead, having another baby became the focus of our lives, and after a long 18 months we were finally pregnant again and afraid that we'd suffer another loss. After a nearly perfect pregnancy, movement stopped, and I drove myself to the hospital steeling my mind against my innermost fears. What if there was another problem? Sadly, my worries came true...our beautiful baby had died.

We named him Brennan William. Life was never to be the same again. My world fell apart. I had never felt so alone and empty, despite the loving presence of my beloved husband. As a mission-driven person, I could not just go back to my previous work (teaching adults and children and also working on my MBA.) Instead, I learned everything I could about miscarriage, stillbirth, infant death, and grief—something I had hoped to avoid but quickly learned had become my intimate companion—and I began offering workshops and writing on the subject, all with the goal of making it better for others. You see, we did not make very good decisions in the middle of our loss—no pictures, no footprints, no clothing, no family ever saw him but us, and we told people not to come to the small ritual we held for him. If we had only known! During the months after Brennan's death, I wrote a book, *Empty Arms: Coping with Miscarriage, Stillbirth and Infant Death* and with others began to develop a national nonprofit for these special

16

families — the former Pregnancy and Infant Loss Center (PILC) in Minneapolis, Minnesota.

David cared deeply. He loved our baby and me, and surely had his share of pain and heartache; he just didn't handle it in the same way I did. He was always more private and quiet. Yet, he too wanted to make it better for others and supported me in all my endeavors to reach out through writing and speaking engagements over the years. During those years we cried lots of tears, had our struggles, came to agree on some things, and definitely agreed to disagree on others. It's been over twenty-five years now; we are thankful to have two wonderful living sons, Kellan and Trevor, and to have been married for over 30 years.

Since those early days I have come to realize that a child's death does not bring good into our life; it is what we do afterward that can bring more good and love into the world. Writing this booklet and sharing our story is meant as a gift of support to you as you make your way toward a 'new normal' in your relationship with each other. Remember why you are together as a couple. By working on your closeness, communication, and compassion for each other, you can strengthen your relationship. I have heard from literally thousands of couples who have done such a thing. But of course it wasn't easy; little that really matters is. You are both worth it, and surely your child would want nothing less for you and your family.

Tim   Monica and I married right out of college and spent the first years of our lives together focusing on careers, buying our first house, and traveling. After several years, we decided it was time to start a family. It never occurred to either of us that life doesn't always go exactly as planned. It took us over two years of temperature taking, on-demand sex, and trips to the doctor with specimen jars tucked under our arm to protect them from Minnesota wind chills, before finally getting pregnant.

That first pregnancy was a difficult roller coaster of emotions. We found out early on we were expecting twins, but were told six weeks later that one of the babies was not viable. Because

Monica never actually miscarried, there was concern that the surviving baby would be at risk at birth. In the end, we had a healthy little girl, and we once again thought we held our future in the palm of our hands.

But, reality reared its ugly head two years later. At the end of a nearly perfect second pregnancy, Monica went to a routine pre-delivery office visit, only to be told the doctor could not detect a heartbeat. Twelve hours after that discovery, our daughter, Kathleen, was born still. There was no known reason for her death and no family history of pregnancy problems. While feeling as though we were the only two people in the world to ever have this happen to them, a mutual acquaintance put us in touch with Sherokee, who was just beginning her work with the Pregnancy and Infant Loss Center (PILC).

In the years that followed, we developed a close friendship with Sherokee and David that grew from our mutual volunteer efforts to raise awareness about perinatal loss. Eventually, I became president of the board of directors of PILC, and our lives overlapped both personally and professionally.

Today, Monica and I have four living children with 10 years between the oldest and youngest. Our marriage has not been without difficulty, but we continue to build on what we've learned about communicating and growing together rather than apart, and we are forever astounded by how much we still don't know.

Hearing the news

Sherokee   When I learned that Brennan had died, I became very self-centered — thinking of him, my sadness, and my emptiness. All I could think about was my precious child. Nothing else mattered. I couldn't believe it, and I went deep inside myself. David, my partner, my love, and Brennan's dad was hardly on my radar screen. I wanted him there; I needed him. Yet, I was overcome by my protective mother emotions for Brennan, not David's pain or needs. I feel badly about that now, years later, but the truth is the truth. It was not fair, and I was in shock!

I replayed the previous few days and wondered what I had done to cause this or what I could have done to prevent it. Feeling responsible is natural; as parents, and particularly as the mother, it was my job to protect this baby. How did this happen? Why did I fail? What did I miss that could have saved our baby? And I worried that not only would I blame myself, but so would everyone else.

While in the hospital and in the early hours and days, I couldn't make decisions, everything seemed so out of control. All that was left to control were my emotions, so I worked on that. I depended on David to tell me what to do. That wasn't really fair. It often didn't help, because he didn't know what I wanted, which resulted in some decisions we both regretted.

I wish I would have been able to find the strength to trust my own instincts. They were there at times, yet I pushed them aside and came to regret some within days. If only I had listened to my heart! For example, the camera was in the car and I asked him if we should get it. He said, "No, why would we?" Instantly, I dismissed the thought only to wish I could rewind the clock. We have no picture of Brennan, and we never will. That makes me incredibly sad. Other parents have wished they would have held their baby longer (or at all) in the hospital or brought the baby home for private time together before saying the final goodbye. I share those regrets, which impacted our relationship and my life over time. Either I had to blame myself (again!) or David. Neither helped us get along better. These days I try harder to forgive myself and David sooner, believing that we did the best we could at the time.

I remember we talked about calling the pastor who married us. David dialed and then proceeded to collapse in tears, unable to speak. Miraculously, at that moment I felt a surge of strength. I asked for the phone and briefly told Don our story. He came immediately. Helping David make that call at a time when I felt like a puddle on the floor gave me some hope. Hope that maybe as a couple we could make it if we had some 'give and take' in our relationship. I hung on to that thought over the tension-filled weeks and months. I believe it was pivotal in our journey. While he comforted me on a daily basis, I was able to console him some of the time, which felt good. When one is receiving the support continuously, without participating in the giving, it becomes one-sided. The receiver can easily spiral down into the puddle of being needy and feeling worthless at the same time.

I suggest that you consider allowing your partner to give you support some of the time, just as soon as you can. Both of you are treading water and both may feel stronger at certain moments to hold the other up. Don't be the hero and try to do it all.

Tim I was at the office when I got the call from Monica telling me that there might be something wrong with the baby. She was at her obstetrician's office for her weekly check when they were unable to find a heartbeat. Some of my first words were, "We'll be okay. Remember, we can handle anything." Looking back, I see that I immediately felt the need to take control of an uncontrollable situation. My words were meant to reassure myself just as much as I wanted to reassure Monica. On the drive to the doctor's office, I was in a daze. My mind raced as I tried to figure out what our lives were going to be like if the baby was indeed dead. I planned who would need to be called, what I was going to say, and how I was going to act once I arrived and saw Monica for the first time.

When the radiologist confirmed that the baby had died, Monica immediately started to cry. I stood silently. After a few moments I turned to the doctor and asked what we were supposed to do next? I needed to stay on task...on schedule, and make sure we did everything that was expected of us. I even recall being concerned what people were going to think if we got too upset about all of this, even though I felt like someone was slowly ripping my heart out of my chest. I could not let down my guard, because if I did my world would crumble.

After speaking to the doctor and deciding that Monica should be admitted to the hospital so labor could be induced, we called our priest. He informed us that he was too busy to come over but that we should feel free to just let the hospital handle everything. Monica decided she needed to go home for a little while and gather some things for her hospital stay. I didn't want to leave. I just wanted everything to end as fast as possible, and going home would only delay the unavoidable.

I have talked to many men over the years who had similar reactions to mine when first hearing the news that there was a problem with their baby. The need to stay in control is a defense mechanism that is real and not done out of a lack of caring or sensitivity. When in shock and dealing with intense emotional pain, all any of us can do is draw on the resources that have been acquired during our life up to that point. Obviously, those resources vary greatly from individual to individual, and rarely do men and women share the same history or socialization process.

Guys, try to think through the ramifications of some of your initial instincts and be open to listening to your partner's perspective. Ladies, try not to jump to conclusions about what your partner's behaviors mean. It's not unlike observing a mighty and serene mountain from a distance, unaware of the smoldering volcano that is hidden within.

Navigating the storm

Sherokee He looked so beautiful, so perfect, even in death. This was my beloved baby. I was proud of him! There were lots of tears, yet surprisingly a few smiles emerged when I saw our first son. I saw him through a mother's loving eyes. This was our beloved baby who had been alive. He was still our beloved baby who happened to have died.

We both spent a few minutes with Brennan after he died and are thankful for that. Sadly, I did not have the strength to fight for the things my heart desired, and I was not sure I should desire them—such things as pictures, the desire to show Brennan off to family and friends, to dress him, bathe him, and take in his scent. Fear, and not knowing what was normal, kept me from making the most of those minutes and hours while in the hospital. Instead, I was filled with regrets of all the things I could have done to make beautiful and special memories. There is so little for me to hold onto now.

No matter how, when, or where your baby died, if you have not yet made some decisions, look within yourself and ask what you 'really' want and need. Trust your instincts, and do what seems important to do even if it is not what your partner wants to do. Learn about your options, agree that you might each need different things, and communicate as best as you can. Minimize regrets as you cope over time. Respect that you each have your own needs and methods of coping. This way you need not be angry with your partner for making decisions that weren't 'right' for you. Be aware that some- times it is fear that motivates decision-making. Many couples later admitted that they held deep regrets because of how the fears influ- enced them.

If you are already past this phase in your loss, then work towards understanding, patience, and forgiveness. Some things cannot be changed, but your attitude about them can be. You did the best you could. Is it time now to move forward together?

Tim   As a few hours passed, I went from trying to rush everything, to wanting to stop time completely. As I adjusted to what was happening, I became more comfortable with the status quo and started to fear how I would react once the baby was born. I could not imagine seeing and holding our child, yet having to say good-bye, within such a short period of time. Monica had moments when she started questioning whether the doctors had made an error in their diagnosis and believed that there was still a chance the baby was alive. She wondered aloud whether she should stop the medication that was starting her labor, thinking it may be harmful to the baby. It upset me to hear her ask these questions, and I grew impatient. I needed her to stay in touch with reality.

When the baby's birth was imminent, I became physically sick and knew that I was reaching the breaking point. My mind raced, my stomach turned, and my breathing was shallow and rapid. When Monica finally asked me to say a prayer with her, I lost control. I shook and sobbed and felt as though I would never stop. Because I had never cried in front of Monica in our seven years of marriage, I feared what her reaction was going to be and was shocked at how good it felt to have her comfort me. She didn't laugh at me, or push me away in disgust, or lose total control of herself. In fact, I saw strength in her I had not experienced before.

Once I released my emotions, I felt rejuvenated and, for the first time since hearing the news, truly believed that we were going to be okay...that together we actually could survive.

When it was time to move to the delivery room, I found myself struck by how similar, yet different, this birth was compared to Emily's (our first child). The delivery room was so familiar. The same doctor was present. The nurses stood in their customary spots. But the sense of excitement and anticipation that filled the air the first time was replaced by a silent foreboding that seemed to hang heavily over the room. Rather than an event, it was a task that needed to be completed. Rather than an experience to celebrate, it was a moment to survive. After Kathleen's birth, the nurses wrapped her in a blanket and carefully weighed her and took hand and foot prints. The feelings of déjà vu brought some comfort, but the silence was haunting. When she was finally handed to me, I was overwhelmed with how perfect she seemed but how dead she felt. I didn't dare let myself bond too much, because I knew that the goodbyes would follow shortly. I believed the longer I spent with her, the more difficult those final moments with her would be, so I rushed both Monica and myself to let go and say goodbye in an effort to try and control the pain.

My need to rush things was my way of trying to navigate the storm without being shipwrecked. Guys, you may understand this. The hours between first hearing that our baby was dead until the time our daughter was handed to me wrapped in that blanket, were probably the most confusing hours of my life. I would alternate between having my mind race with fear and anticipation to totally numbing myself to the reality of what was happening. Remarkably, for the most part, I came off to others as simply being subdued. I wish I had known then that my feelings were normal, and that I did indeed have a right to feel out of control.

After all these years, these are the hours about which I have the most regrets. While I know I was doing the best I could under the circumstances, it bothers me still that I pushed my feelings on Monica and convinced her to make decisions she almost certainly would not otherwise have made.

You may have noticed that Sherokee wrote above that you should trust your initial instincts and go with them. I, on the other hand, suggest you be cautious of those immediate gut feelings. Ask yourself whether they are really what is best for you and your partner long-term, or if you are attempting to justify choices that let you off the hook in the short-term. Whenever possible, make joint decisions, talk to each other, and use the time well. Know that feeling out of control is very normal. What is happening (or what did happen) is truly not something you could have stopped, and it's okay to acknowledge that truth. If it is past the decision-making time and you have regrets, express them to your partner and work on reminding yourself that you did the best you could under very difficult circumstances. While nothing can rewrite history, what we learn from situations like those, and how we respond going forward, are some of the greatest gifts our children's short lives offer us.

Funeral, memorials, cremation, burial

Sherokee Why have a funeral for a tiny baby? Is it even an option? I didn't know the answers and was incapable at the time of doing the research. I asked David and a friend who worked at the hospital to help with this. My inclination was to do what was quick, easy, and inexpensive. Oh, how I regret that now. David talked me out of hospital disposition, for which I am quite thankful. However, we planned on having a small service just for ourselves, though we told a few relatives and some showed up. Were we trying to make it easier on each other? On them? I'm not sure, but we definitely did not do that one well.

My family listened to me and didn't come, so they never saw Brennan, in person or in a picture, and they were not at the one ceremony that included him. Thankfully, a few of David's relatives did come, and over the years we have expressed our gratitude.

We cremated Brennan and scattered his ashes in a river. That meant we had no special cemetery to go to be with him. This is something many parents, especially mothers, seem to do often—visit the grave and in a unique sort of way, continue to 'parent' their baby on holidays, anniversaries, and sometimes just ordinary days when they want to be near their baby. Many mothers who live in cold climates have commented to me that they are upset about their baby being in the cold ground. They wish they could 'warm' them up. Not a rational thought, but a real concern shared by many.

I have heard stories of dads, or other relatives, planning the services to protect mom from the heartache. Usually the mothers, while grateful, wished they had more say. While both parents should be included and involved, that may or may not have been the case. If this is behind you, talk through why decisions were made and any regrets. Work through this rather than hold it in, or resentment may build.

Talk with your partner about what you need to do on an ongoing basis regarding spending time with your baby either at the cemetery or if you have the ashes. Some parents create a special area in their home where they put a picture or two, a memento, and the ashes for awhile. Others find the need to put the ashes away to be brought out on days when one or the other wants to hold the baby's remains and remember. You may have different wishes about how to do this. Since most people your age haven't made decisions yet about your own final disposition plan, making one for your baby seems out of order and can be difficult. Attempt to honor your partner's needs and ask him/her to honor yours if they are different.

Tim   Because our church so completely let us down, we found ourselves not knowing how to go about planning a memorial service. The unspoken message we had received from the priest was that this event was not worth his time, so I questioned whether a funeral was even appropriate. What would people think? Would anyone come? If they didn't come, how could I handle the rejection? If they did come, would I make a total fool of myself? Due to my fears, I could not even handle the thought of participating in the planning of a service. Monica took over that task and I simply showed up, remembering very little about it when it was over. Looking back, I wish we had done more. It was our chance to let our family meet Kathleen, see how much we loved her, and let them share in our sorrow—which would have undoubtedly helped lighten our load.

I envy the dads who have shared their stories with me of planning and participating in the memorial service that was held for their baby. I get angry when I think how our priest failed us in so many ways and cannot help but wonder what might have been if he had responded differently. But, I do not allow myself to feel beat up with regrets. It does no good, and no decision I did or did not make was any reflection on my love for

Kathleen. I was in survival mode, operating on adrenaline with a determination to put one foot in front of the other. If I had not cared so much, none of it would have been so difficult.

———————————

Because of our unique circumstances in how our priest responded to our loss, I do not believe that my reaction to planning and participating in a memorial service is all that common. But, if nothing else, I think what I shared above points to the vital part a caregiver plays when helping a family through a traumatic crisis. A caring and professional nurse, doctor, social worker, funeral director, or clergy plays a pivotal role as to whether a family moves ahead with good memories that bring comfort and healing, or whether they struggle with anger and bitterness, even years later.

Hours and days later

Sherokee I would rather have traded places with my child. I would have given my life that he might live. How do you explain that to someone else? David couldn't imagine the thought of losing me and didn't like it when I said that. But truly, I believe most mothers and some fathers have felt this way. Focusing primarily on the baby may not be easily understood by dad. He is protective and may be more focused on mom. Although a father named Ryan did point out that he felt focused on both mom and baby saying, "I just wanted to make it all better for both my daughter and my wife. I would have done anything to take away the pain for both of them."

In an effort to provide comfort and hope, many fathers, or other family members, may say things like, "I am so thankful you are alive," or "We/you can have another baby in time." This doesn't sit well with some of us. Another baby isn't what we want; we want this baby. In their heart of hearts, I think those offering this advice know that and agree, but after many hours at the 'hardware store' searching for the right tool or a nugget of loving advice, they may resort to such things—

which can inadvertently be great argument starters.

Building a cocoon to climb into and hide was one of my early coping mechanisms. A phrase I repeated over and over was, "If I could just go to sleep for a year, then when I woke up I'd feel better." Yet, sleeping was something I found difficult most of the time. I tried many things—music, visualization, praying, walking, drinking warm milk or tea with honey—often with little success.

Then in the morning, I found that getting out of bed was almost impossible. I was exhausted, tired, and down. My energy level was low. What was there to get up for, to live for? I had no other children at the time, and David was off at work after a few days. Soon the flowers died and the cards stopped coming. The isolation and days of talking with no one affected me. Previous priorities and important life events were no longer of any consequence. They simply didn't matter. Nothing much mattered. The darkness was all encompassing. The shock was numbing in some ways and surrealistic in others. All my energy went toward taking breaths, crying, and remembering every detail of Brennan's pregnancy and birth— his short little life. I kept replaying it over and over. Mostly asking why? This is what I needed, and I am thankful David supported me in this, though I know it became difficult for him over time. I suppose the post pregnancy hormonal changes I was going through didn't help my coping and my mood.

Dealing with the baby's room was something we did rather soon. My mom and I took care of cleaning it out. It seemed like the women's responsibility, and I wondered if it was a bit early to do this. However, in a way it was a relief to have it done. I did keep out his teddy bear and a few favorite blankets and outfits I had sewn. These became my comfort items to cuddle when I needed my 'Brennan fix.' Thankfully, no one tried to do this without me. It was my job, and I needed to do it on my timetable. I know of many families who kept their baby's room up for a long time. If it was too difficult to walk by each day, they closed the door. Yet, it became a refuge for good memories, hope-filled moments, and sad reminders.

Being tired and having feelings much like depression are common. If you have previous experience with depression, you may find this extra troubling and may want others to keep an eye on you (since it is difficult to see yourself clearly when you are in the middle of it).

Following the loss, the grief responses and the inability to get back to a regular life may be viewed by others as a serious problem. They may not understand the normal feelings of craziness and depression. There may be a rush to medicate. One mother said she wanted to create bumper stickers that said, "I'm not crazy, I'm grieving." In **For the Love of Angela***, Nancy Mayer-Whittington writes, "Grief, like so many experiences, is not to be rushed, not to be pushed aside, nor to be taken lightly. Grief in varying stages, lasts a lifetime." Grief is hard work and needs to be done the hard way with all the emotions that go with it. Jump in, go with the flow, and believe that though there will be a few steps forward and many steps backward, over time and by doing your grief work, you will feel better, finding hope and health again.*

<u>*While I had feelings of wanting to go to sleep or even die, I didn't really mean it. However, there are some who do mean it. If you seriously have a plan to end your life or to hurt someone else, it is imperative that you tell someone. You need immediate help. Please call your partner, a friend, a relative, or 911 if you are close to actually doing something. Your child and family do not want you to hurt this much. Take this seriously, and call if ever you have thoughts of specific harmful actions and a plan in your mind.*</u>

Tim　　Monica came home from the hospital the day our daughter Emily turned two-years-old. The next day was the family birthday party at our house. While the need to keep up a good front was comforting for me in many ways, it was during that time I realized Monica and I were going to grieve very differently. The initial shock was wearing off and reality was starting to set in. We were home—but without our baby.

Without asking Monica, I woke up early that first morning home and took down Kathleen's crib. I put it in the attic and hoped that by stuffing it away...along with my feelings...that life would return to normal.

It didn't. Taking down the crib was the cause of our first big disagreement since Kathleen's birth. Monica felt cheated, and I was insulted that she questioned my judgment or motives. I think I knew at the time that I blew it, but I was not about to admit it at that point.

Not only did that decision cause tension, it ultimately added to the layers of insecurity that were rapidly building up inside me. I already questioned my ability to protect my family, and now I felt guilty for not being a more sensitive husband. It was a lonely and frightening time.

Returning to work right away and mowing the lawn three times a week when I was at home were other seemingly good remedies for my pain. After all, people were telling me that if I kept busy and moved on, everything would be fine. What they failed to tell me was that I would cry in the shower every morning, then again on my way to work, and often on my way home. In an attempt to keep my masculinity intact, I never shared any of those emotional moments with Monica. In fact, I actually grew more and more impatient with her tears and got out my 'toolbox' to try and fix her. I can see now that I most likely came off to Monica as if I didn't care or that I had moved on. My outward behavior was clearly not indicative of what I was feeling.

It really wasn't until we started going to a support group...not my idea...that I realized I was not the only husband/father on the planet struggling and coping the way I did. It was amazing how much of a difference that little piece of knowledge helped me open up and talk about my feelings.

When I re-read what I wrote above, I wonder how I could have been such a jerk. But, the reality is, much of what I had been taught about being a boy, man, husband, and father up to that point, impacted how I reacted. "Big boys don't cry." "Just shake it off, you're fine." "Once you lose control of the game, it's over." "I promise to love, honor, and protect."

What I learned as time went on was that if I just let Monica talk through her feelings, she felt much better and was able to move to other activities. To my amazement, what I learned was that it was not because she expected answers that she shared her thoughts with me, she just needed to process her feelings by sharing them out loud. I credit the book *Men Are From Mars, Women Are From Venus*, for my eventual enlightenment.

There was certainly a part of me that simply wanted our lives to return to normal once we were home from the hospital and the initial shock was gone. Putting away the crib, rushing back to work, and pretending that our dinner conversation should be as relaxed as two weeks previous, were all ways that I attempted to make our lives and routines the same as they were before Kathleen died. It really wasn't until our support group leader referred to our 'new normal' that it clicked with me...I had been changed forever.

Other children at home

Sherokee Sometimes the distraction and love for other children can help soften the blow and give purpose to days that otherwise might be spent in bed. And other times, those other children get in the way of necessary grieving. Since we had no living children, we had no experience with living siblings. This was bittersweet since the house was so empty and there were no distractions of children to dull the pain and keep us busy. However, I do know of many families who found themselves resenting their other children at times. They wanted their 'perfect' baby back, not a whiny, cranky sister or brother. The effort to meet the needs of the living children was wearing. Food needed to be made, dishes done, clothes washed, errands run, carpooling, and homework accomplished. Yet, there can be those loving times when holding a child and showing love warms one's heart.

Tim Monica and I were lucky that we were in agreement as to how to handle our communication with 2-year-old Emily. She was very verbal and asked a lot of questions that we tried to answer with as much clarity as possible in words she could understand. On a couple of occasions we shared more information than she was asking for, or could comprehend, and we quickly saw that we had gone too far.

Of course, we had also lost our innocence. We knew that children could die, and we were both terrified something might happen to Emily. Because Monica got pregnant only three months after Kathleen's death, I was also consumed with fear of having another loss and went about the task of rebuilding my protective wall.

It was not long before Emily started teaching us more about grieving than any support group, priest, or counselor. Her matter-of-fact acceptance of Kathleen's death was as refreshing as her unquestioning love for the sister she never saw. When Emily accidentally came across the photos of Kathleen that we had avoided showing her, she looked right through the discolored skin and appearance of death, and instead saw a "bootiful baby" who she was very excited to call her sister.

Whether you agree, or not, as to how open to be with your other children about the details of your baby's death, do not shut the kids out of your grief. Kids need to learn that sadness and tears are okay. They are by-products of love. Besides, no matter how hard you try, or how clever you think you are being, children almost never fail to sense sadness and tension in their parents.

Baby or older child – grieving for our different dreams

Sherokee In our minds, we each held onto dreams that were unique. In the case of our Brennan, we learned much later that David and I were often on different wavelengths. I thought of him as the baby he was, and I missed the rocking, nursing, cooing, and cuddling. An older child was not yet in my thoughts. First, I needed to experience, and sadly, say goodbye to those precious baby moments I had long awaited. A baby was the focus of my dreams. David, on the other hand, did not feel as comfortable with babies, and that wasn't the ultimate dream he had. His plans revolved around enjoying activities with his children such as fishing, camping, and coaching.

Most dads I know have shared that holding and rocking a baby was not the main picture they had of their child. Usually dads have an older child in their mind's eye. As we approached Brennan's 5th birthday, I distinctly remember David paying more attention than any previous birthday, except the first one. The fifth appeared to be a significant birthday for him. In fact, he made a point of asking how we would celebrate the day; he talked of the things a five-year-old might be doing. Moved to tears, he seemed to be missing his son and those projected times of playing catch, tossing him in the air, and wrestling. His picture of Brennan was focused there, at five and older, mine was not. I still missed my baby Brennan.

Be mindful that you may be grieving for the loss of different dreams (at least the hopes and plans you had for your children), and over time the reminders of what might have been may bring sadness and intense emotions at different times for each of you. It might be helpful to talk over those hopes of your child and at what stage or age you seem to focus on. Were you dreaming of a special experience or event to come—maybe fishing with a toddler, first communion, graduation, or even a wedding?

Tim In so many ways, Kathleen is my forever baby. I picture her as she looked at birth and don't find myself being able to put a face on her as she would look today. However, I definitely find the "milestone" birthdays to be the most difficult. I felt so cheated the year she would have started school...when she would have had that "sweet 16th" birthday...or walked down the aisle for graduation. When her older sister was married, I found myself being sad that Emily was not able to have her as her maid of honor, and wondered what Kathleen would have looked like in those beautiful lavender dresses. I believe there is a tendency to think that everyone, especially our partner, envisions our thoughts and dreams in the same way we do...and it's only when we dare share those thoughts that we realize how different our images really are. Over the years, I have found this to be a source of misunderstanding, because I simply don't think to say out loud how I see Kathleen in my mind's eye. I assume everyone sees her as I do.

When those moments of thinking about your baby come out of nowhere...no matter how long it has been since the death...do not try and avoid them or push them away. As life moves forward and the pain becomes less intense, those times can actually be very comforting. I referred earlier to my thoughts of Kathleen on Emily's wedding day. What I didn't share was that those feelings came to me, literally, as I was starting to walk Emily down the aisle. The maid of honor (Emily's best friend) was in front of us. As I watched her, it dawned on me that I had been harboring some anger toward this girl all day. While I had not given it much thought...chalking it up to father-of-the-bride jitters... it hit me that I wanted Kathleen to be that beautiful woman walking in front of us. I cannot deny that I was unprepared for having those thoughts, but I was very grateful that Kathleen was there with me in my heart as we made our way to the altar.

The way we grieve – 'to be fixed or not,' that is the question.

Sherokee If David would have asked me, and I would have had the words, I might have told him. "I don't want to be fixed! I am broken and I cannot be fixed! At least not now." Maybe someday God would use His power to make me whole again, maybe not. The grieving I needed to do was how I mothered this baby. It was how I kept Brennan alive in my heart and how I had the courage to continue living. It was also how I kept my first baby Marama in my heart, since I realized I also was grieving for her, too. While I wanted to be consoled, I could not be fixed.

I thought about Brennan all the time—remembering, sharing with others, weeping, and sometimes sitting in the puddle of my pain. In the early days and weeks, wallowing is what helped me the most, thinking about what happened, and how I felt. I found comfort in both the sadness and the beautiful reminders of love. Sometimes I even felt his kicks—called phantom kicks—that in a strange sort of way did keep me connected to him. I also did everything I could to control things in my life, a difficult goal given the 'Swiss cheese mind' and absent-mindedness that had taken over my once organized one. I had lost control of my pregnancy and the outcome, but it wasn't long before I found a more 'active' way to accept my son's death and start to do things like collect more baby mementos and decide to publish my own book...so it wouldn't be controlled by some publisher who might not keep it alive for years and years.

These were my ways of coping— the only things I knew to do at the time. As a little girl, I always knew I could cry and be emotional. It came naturally, and I could not have stopped it even if I wanted to. And when in crisis, I sought more control and action. Thus, I was *doing* something by being fully engaged in my experience, which allowed me that chance to *be* in it, too

I often wondered why David tried so hard to make me better? At times, I resented that he tried every tool in the tool shed in an attempt to lift my spirits. It didn't make any sense to me then. He worked to fix, console, and protect me. Now that I see men's need to *fix* and to *do* something, I think I have become more understanding that it was done out of his love for me. If I had only known then that this was his natural tendency.

Our different wavelengths got in the way sometimes. I wanted a partner to be available to talk about the experience with me, and before long he wanted to help me move toward finding happiness again. Why shouldn't I cry— for a long time and often? Why shouldn't I review the experience of the pregnancy, the death, and what I was doing to change the system? Obviously, I wanted to be on my timetable, not his or anyone else's. Oh, but that was so hard to admit to myself, let alone tell others that was what I needed to do.

This is one of the most common issues that couples share as a source of tension and misunderstanding. One bereaved father of a miscarried baby talked openly saying, "If I had known that all my ex-wife really wanted was for me to sit with her in her pain and listen, offering a few nods, hugs, and affirmations, I don't know if we'd be separated right now. Instead, I tried everything I could to make her better, cheer her up, and get her to move on towards having another baby and seeking happiness. How wrong I was in my understanding of her needs and how hard I made it for myself as I tried to help her."

Sorrow is painful. When you love someone who is deeply hurting, it is natural to wish to help them feel better and to protect them from such pain. This is about love and care. But this experience is so deep and painful that one really can't be fixed. If you don't want to be fixed, say so. A treasure has been lost and no words or deeds will take the sorrow away. The tough journey must be taken. There is no magic cure and no tools from any store that will fix such deep pain. Neither of you can magically make it better, so let go of that pressure.

Tim I found it difficult when Monica seemed to be sad for too long. I was impatient and didn't allow myself to be overly sympathetic. I honestly don't believe it had anything to do with being insensitive or uncaring, because I secretly cried when I was alone. But I needed control. I needed to start to feel like I could survive. When Monica was sad, I felt myself going backwards and either lashed out or withdrew because I thought I was losing the battle. These same feelings caused me to try and fix her. I offered solutions to help her stop from being sad because it was my way of convincing myself that we would both be okay. I also truly believed that when she shared her feelings and questions she was looking to me for answers. It was simply my role to try and protect and make my family heal. While I couldn't stop Kathleen's death from happening, I could pull us along and lead us out of our mire of sadness. Or so I thought.

In the years since Kathleen's death, I've learned to try and be more sympathetic when Monica is down or stressed and attempt to only listen without saying much...something I have to consciously force myself to do. My natural reaction is still to try and offer practical solutions in order to make the sorrow or tension go away.

Being able to openly communicate with the one you love seems like it should be a simple task, but often it is not. Even after 30+ years of marriage, I'm still not a great talker, but in a pinch, I have learned to be a heck of a listener. I have become so comfortable with it that I actually kind of enjoy it. Whether your hesitancy to share your feelings with your partner is due to fear of making yourself vulnerable, or simply a belief that she should be able to know how you are feeling, understand that she will likely cherish your willingness to open up. But it is just as important to learn to be the one who can simply sit there, listen, nod, and say, "uh huh." Remember, talking is only half of the equation that makes communication effective. Without someone to listen, it loses something — not to mention that the person talking looks as if they are a little crazy.

Active grieving, active listening

Sherokee Many women, and some men, need to actively grieve, spend time in the mire and/or do something special, something 'active' to honor their baby. It is a way to grieve, not what keeps us from the grief. And when in that anguish, we like to have others who will listen. That means silence and a few affirming comments like, "That's okay," or "Uh huh." I know such simple responses seemed inadequate to David who cared so much and tried so hard. When he used this type of active listening, without offering solutions, it helped me because I felt that he shared my pain as I worked to 'weave our baby's memories into the fabric of our life.' When he didn't, I became frustrated.

These days I do feel badly that I did not really honor David's style of coping and his needs. Selfishly, I expected he would join me in the valley of my pain, which he did much of the time in those early days. As I learned something new or wrote about another part of the journey in my book, I wanted to talk with him about it. This must have made him weary, but I didn't see it. I was in my deep canyon, doing my work. His patience with me was tremendous. Yet, now I wonder when and how did he really grieve in his own manner? I don't think I really listened to him or picked up on his cues. Did he delay his work until he knew I would survive this? If I had been more understanding of his process and needs, might he have had an easier time?

To bereaved mom Wendy, who helped comfort others and made baby gowns to donate to the hospital, active grieving was necessary in order to heal her wound, a bit like draining an infection. To her husband, listening and watching that 'draining' was painful...his family's style of coping with pain was to leave it alone, 'Don't pick the scab; let it heal on its own.' (read more about their story in the Differing Perspectives section)

Understand your style of coping, then communicate it to your partner. If you take some time to examine what you are doing and how it makes you feel, you will have some idea about your style. Are you an outward griever or do you prefer to keep it to yourself? Do you need to 'actively' write, volunteer, comfort others, or spend time with music as you feel and heal? Can you get back into work or not? Do you prefer to read books or talk with others in support groups within your religious community, or even in a chat room on the internet? Keep talking with each other as you explore and cope, and don't let denial or being 'strong' get in the way of your communication.

Tim 'Active grieving' is a tricky concept. While some people may be freer to show how they are coping by crying and talking about their feelings, I was one of those who camouflaged my 'active grieving.' Unlike some men, I have no desire to build things or tear my car apart, but I really get off having my lawn look good. So, in those weeks following Kathleen's death, I had the best groomed yard in St. Paul. Not only did I need the physical exercise to relieve some of my stress, I had a strong need to do something that had a beginning and an end. I had an even greater desire to do something well. And while those factors were big reasons why I mowed non-stop, I will also admit that I simply wanted to be alone. It was while being physically active that I could talk with Kathleen in my mind. I could tell her I was sorry for the things I screwed up, as well as share with her how much I loved her and missed her. And the beauty of it all was that, to the rest of the world, I simply looked like a guy with a lawn fetish. Unfortunately, that is the way I looked to Monica, as well. I knew she was hurt and angry that I seemed to be distancing myself, but it never occurred to me to try and explain what was going on in my head. Until she read this manuscript, I doubt if I had ever communicated to her what I was doing during that time. The innate desire to retreat when I'm stressed is one of those concepts I find difficult to explain. Yet, the concept is so simple in my mind's eye that I wonder how Monica cannot instinctively know why it is necessary.

---

*One way I actively grieved was to focus my energies on areas of competency I felt comfortable with. Believe it or not, my talents include more than being a lawn mower – at least in my opinion. Being a former journalism student, I wrote a newspaper article that was later published as a booklet entitled, **A Father's Story**. I also used my business background to become involved with the board of directors of the Pregnancy and Infant Loss Center, which Sherokee was instrumental in founding. While I was not necessarily sitting around talking about how sad or angry I was, I definitely channeled that energy into something that helped relieve my sense of helplessness.*

Pressure and 'help' from others

Sherokee Fighting the pressure from others was a daily battle in the early weeks and months. How could anyone, even David sometimes, suggest it was time to go out and have some fun? How could I possibly attend baptisms and baby showers? Holidays would never be the same again, yet I was expected to put up a good front. If I wanted to stay in my cocoon, why couldn't I? I got up many mornings, somehow managing to fix breakfast, pay bills, or even make a few phone calls. What more did I need to do to prove I could live through this? I didn't like the pressure I felt from others, but I didn't want to tell them how hard it was to fulfill their expectations of me.

I missed meetings, forgot to do things I needed to do, and moved from one room to another wondering why I had gone there in the first place. I felt as though I was going crazy, and I didn't want to tell anyone how bad it was. So I put up a front, made excuses when I couldn't go places, and hid in the bedroom during the early holidays to avoid a scene.

Pressure will come sooner than you may be ready for it — pressure to get up, move on, and do something productive. Some pressure is not all bad; it can motivate you to try a little harder when you don't feel like trying at all. Yet, indeed, if you still find it too difficult to attend certain functions or go to parties or social events, it's okay to hold back for a while. Putting up a front in public is painful to do. This is especially so when it involves being around children the age of yours, or even children at all. Now if the pressure comes from your partner, you may be even less tolerant of the comments. Discuss the difficulties you are having. Compromise sometimes if you can, and stick to your guns if you really can't. Again, communication is critical here.

Tim I was much more in tune to what I thought our friends and family expected of us than Monica seemed to be. She really didn't care. I did. My fear was that our feelings were not justified and that our grief could be perceived as being strange or abnormal. I didn't want to come off to the world as being weak...especially since I already felt vulnerable as a man who had failed. While putting these thoughts on paper today seems almost ridiculous, at the time the feelings were real. I was torn between understanding that it was okay to take time to grieve but not understanding the difference between healthy grief and being stuck in grief.

As is the case with many young parents, this was my first experience with deep personal loss. The only thing I understood was that my world seemed to be falling apart, and yet others acted like it should be no big deal. Every time someone compassionately asked how my wife was doing, it reinforced the idea that while they may understand HER pain, they certainly didn't understand MINE. All these factors influenced me and resulted in my pushing Monica to do things she may not have been ready for. I thought she should attend her sister's baby shower, because I didn't want her to hurt her sister's feelings. I wanted to start socializing with friends sooner than she did, because I thought that if we didn't, they might not ask us again. And when I sensed people were sick of talking about Kathleen and our grief, I attempted to change the subject rather than have them be uncomfortable.

I think this is where many people say, "Everyone has to grieve in their own way." While I don't dispute that at all, I do believe that if there is not some understanding of where each other is at and a willingness to compromise, this can be a source of big trouble for couples. Anything done in excess presents dangers to relationships, and potentially, one's health. After all, if one person decides that 'their way' to cope is to retreat into total solitude while the other feels that socializing at the bar 5 nights a week is 'their way' of surviving, where does the story end? It can be hard work supporting someone when you can't relate to his or her behavior, but try to find a middle ground, which is likely a better spot than either extreme.

Intimacy

Sherokee Intimacy created Brennan. Intimacy would not bring him back. In fact, intimacy reminded me even more of the pain. My recollection is that at times I avoided such closeness with David in the months that followed Brennan's death. I liked being held, and kissing sometimes was acceptable to me, but anything more was too painful. Now I had another thing to feel guilty for—it seemed I was doing my best to complicate our lives and make us hurt even more. My daily feelings were about the baby, what I was missing, and what I was going to do about it. I needed to turn this into something good or I couldn't go on. This kept me busy, often all night—another way to avoid intimacy.

Sexual relations could lead to another baby; that was a scary thought to me. I wasn't even close to wanting another baby on many days. Yet, there were others when I couldn't wait to fill my empty arms. Feeling conflicted was common during those early weeks and months. Eventually, we did become close and intimate again and found ourselves pregnant. That journey was intense and overwhelming at times.

You may have different desires over time. Once again, communication becomes key. Take a look at what you are doing and why. Can you compromise sometimes? If sexual intercourse is too difficult to consider, are there ways you can agree to be close without that level of intimacy? Put on the soft, romantic music, light the candles, and see what happens. Maybe you will find it softens you to the pain and opens you to once again experience the love in your relationship. Find happiness in the moment.

Tim When I am feeling stressed, as though life is out of control, I fluctuate between needing to be held in order to sleep at night to not wanting anyone or anything close to me. Since I rarely knew how I was going to feel on any given day in the weeks following Kathleen's death, it was a pretty tall order to expect Monica to somehow figure it out.

I also had a very hard time talking about when the right time to resume sexual relations might be, even though Monica broached the topic numerous times. To me it was not something I wanted to discuss...I simply wanted it when the mood struck me. (I guess some things never change.)

While I think we both struggled with the accompanying guilt that followed a period of enjoyment and intimacy, I can't recall ever really discussing how we felt about it at the time.

I recommend you learn from my mistakes. In other words, try and be willing to discuss your needs and desires with your partner. Be understanding of the fact that physically it may take time for a woman to be ready for intercourse, but that does not mean she wouldn't like being held. Finally, know that feeling good does not somehow dishonor your baby who died. And if considering a subsequent pregnancy, talk with your physician regarding any questions you have.

Her ongoing needs

Sherokee Once I had exhausted David as my daily listener, I realized I needed others to join me in the journey and the mission. Thankfully, I found them, and I visited with them often. I needed to retell my story over and over, including the birth and what led up to it. I needed to say and hear Brennan's name. This venting was vital. I believe it helped me to reinvest in life sooner—I was incorporating him into my new life by keeping his memory alive.

I needed to make some positives out of this tragedy. I wrote, sent sympathy cards to strangers, and talked on the phone consoling newly bereaved moms into the middle of the night. In a way, I was making lemonade from the lemons I had been given. Turning this into something sweet and helpful to others would eventually bring me less of a sour taste. My excitement about improving care for bereaved families, when shared by others, inspired great plans. This helped me heal...knowing I was doing God's work. At times I would stay up all night writing. At other times I would stay in bed all day, struggling to care about eating, working, my family, or much of anything. I had never done this before and it scared me. This single focus probably got to David after awhile, maybe even driving him 'nuts' at times, but most of the time he didn't interfere. (Of course, I probably still do many things that drive him nuts.) Later he admitted he was worried about me.

I was an active griever; not everyone is. Some people cope best by dwelling, others by allowing the feelings to be there but not focusing so much on the experience like Charmayne and Susan (see their comments in the Differing Perspectives section), and still others by keeping busy doing other things.

I also know that I cried some everyday for at least six months. I know because I counted. Every day. It was what I had to do. This did make me feel better in a strange sort of way. Humor, David's strength, was not mine (ask anyone). Playing, laughing, going out, forgetting, and pretending, were not my ways of moving on. My arms ached for Brennan; it felt like my heart was constantly skipping beats, and I remember sighing all the time. A constant red and raw nose was another sign of how I was handling it all. No one told me how to do this mourning thing. I just did what seemed right at the time. I suppressed my anger, believing I had none, though of course I soon learned that I had fooled myself. I doubted myself, wondering if this was the way to do it. The whole thing made me feel crazy and alone. I honestly didn't know if I was going to make it.

On anniversaries, due dates, and holidays, I needed to include Brennan. I wanted family and friends to remember him. Mother and Father's Day were big days for both of us. Having a plan ahead of time helped tremendously. On his birthdays I made cakes; after our sons Kellan and Trevor came along we sang him "Happy Birthday" and talked about what their older brother would have been like.

I came to realize that I hoped to always have tears for my children who died. While I hardly ever cry now or feel anywhere near as sad, I still hold them all in my heart with love and joy. I hope to always be close to them, to say their names, and to keep their memories alive.

About 5 years after our loss, I learned of bereaved parents Curt and Sue who had a special way of recognizing their baby and honoring each others' feelings. They bought a special candle for their baby

Hope. On any day when one found Hope's candle burning, it was a message to the other to be gentle and understanding. They brought her candle to special holidays and anniversaries. With this symbolism, few words were needed and lots of hugs and special looks were forthcoming. I wish we had thought of this nice, non-verbal communication tool for our use.

Find your way of coping and use it. Discover your partner's way and honor it. Once in awhile step out of yourself and your own process. You can find yourself too caught up in the experience of it and lose who you are. Let your needs be known. If you think about it and look inside, you do know what you need. While you may not have all of them met, you have a better chance at getting support if you give them a voice. Remember, you were happy before; you can work to be happy again. Also, find resources – people, written materials, and even the web – to assist you to better understand mourning and the growth that can take place over time.

His ongoing needs

Tim   Ideally, I probably needed a mind reader as I worked through my grief, because I was not able to verbalize my feelings ... especially to Monica. I had never before experienced such total helplessness, and it wasn't until time had passed that I was even able to begin to understand my own actions. At the time, once the cycle of misunderstanding got rolling, it was nearly impossible to stop it without the help of an objective outside source. It didn't matter whether that assistance came in the form of reading a book about couple communication, going to a support group, or talking to a trusted friend or counselor. We both needed to recognize that our interactions as a couple were not necessarily unique and, most importantly, didn't mean we had a bad relationship. In other words, misery loves company! The more Monica sensed my lack of support, the more hurt and sad she became. The sadder she became, the more I either withdrew or tried to fix her because I couldn't handle seeing her that way.

Once anger became part of the equation, not only did I feel inadequate as a father who could not protect his daughter from death, but also as a husband who didn't effectively support his partner. Just as much as she needed me to acknowledge her sadness, I needed reassurance from her that I was a good father and husband, and that she would at least attempt to understand and accept the fact that I had a hard time expressing my feelings. We BOTH needed to say out loud that despite the fact we didn't understand each other's emotional responses, we didn't question for a moment our love for Kathleen or one another. Agreeing to disagree or trying to set aside a time for both of us to just talk while the other only listened would have been helpful...with the understanding that if I didn't want to talk, she would just let me sit silently and assure me that I was not failing by doing that.

Know that as time moves on, you will likely be learning the one-step-forward and two-steps-backward grief dance. The tricky moves that comprise this little boogie can feel discouraging some days and downright scary on others, not to mention all the toes that will likely get bruised in the process. Understand that it is unlikely your moods will coincide with your partner's, so a willingness to let him/her know how you are feeling on any given day will definitely make this period easier.

Back to work, back to life

Sherokee Prior to Brennan's death I consulted with businesses, teaching classes on self-esteem, assertiveness/aggressiveness, and team building. Such work required a sense of self, purpose, confidence, and an enthusiasm to be the 'up front' facilitator. I loved this work.

Then I had a baby die and could not make myself get out of

bed, get dressed, sell my services, or show up and look confident. Life as I knew it had fallen apart. I was a wreck! The best I could do was to eventually sign up to be a substitute teacher in our school district for a few days that winter. That only required following someone else's plan and attempting to keep order in a classroom of elementary students. It was something to do on the days I could say, "Yes," to the caller from the school. The nice thing was, I could also say, "No," when I needed to, and believe me, I did that quite well.

David, on the other hand, couldn't stand sitting around and needed to get back to work. He dove right back into a full time schedule and began playing basketball again on Tuesdays and hunting on some weekends. He was seeking some normalcy for the both of us, while I was cocooned at home. I don't recall if he was glad to escape the sad world that was now our home, if he felt it was right to go back, or if he felt guilt. I guess it is time to ask him. Funny how 26 years later I realize I can't answer that question because I don't recall ever talking about it. Another testimony to the small, narrow world I was living in at the time.

Of course, practically speaking, at least one of us had to work if we were to eat and pay our mortgage, but that is not anything I thought of at the time. My own little world did not include survival issues such as those. Looking back, thankfully, his world did. However, there were times I would be angry at him for appearing to 'move on.' I resented that he could leave me each day and walk in the door each night wondering what we would do for supper and inquiring about my day. How ordinary! This was a world I seemed to have lost. I thought I needed him to be there with me to feel the sadness, to share the darkness with me, and to remember the positives and the love we had for Brennan. I imagine he thought I should seek more light in my day, sometimes wishing I could find a different focus, like my previous work, since comforting other grieving mothers had overtaken my life and was draining.

I envied him and his ability to do that—to care about some of his previous life—to get up, shower, go to work, accomplish ordinary or extraordinary things, and come home again having survived it all.

After a few months we were able to plan a vacation to Hawaii, our favorite place. It was a bittersweet trip, but it did allow us to escape for a bit, and I do remember having some fun.

Whether you go back to work right away or not, the decision about when to go back will likely come from many who think you need to go back (to keep your mind occupied) or from your employer who needs you back. Often co-workers don't know how to treat you when you do come back and may not speak directly and compassionately to you about your baby's death, or they may ignore the topic completely. They are probably uncomfortable and don't quite know what to say or do. People often focus on mom and ask how she is doing, not how dad is.

Give your boss a heads up that there may be days when you won't be able to make it in to work or won't be very productive. Maybe going back part time for a while or even a week or two of half days could help with the transition. You may need some extra encouragement to take care of yourself. Take breaks when you just can't go on. Ask your boss for flexibility about leaving if you just can't make it through some days. Some women change directions and quit work at such a time as this.

Tim Because I owned my own business, the pressure to return to work did not come from an employer telling me how much time I could take off, but from a business partner who did not completely understand what I was dealing with and customers who needed their work completed. I will also admit that I had a need to get out of the house after being there for a week. I was overwhelmed by the sadness that consumed our home life and the thought of being distracted by work was welcome. Obviously, those feelings brought with them a level of guilt that added to the growing stack of emotions I was stockpiling.

There is no doubt that I was preoccupied with thoughts of Kathleen for weeks after my return, and I was probably not truly productive again for at least six to eight months. It was the first time since starting my business that I had thoughts of walking away from it all and forfeiting the eight years of sweat and money I had invested. It meant nothing to me anymore, and I questioned whether I had the burning desire needed to keep it going. The range of responses I encountered from co-workers and clients was everything from total avoidance to someone telling me that I shouldn't be sad because at least Kathleen wasn't older when she died.

I learned to answer the proverbial, "How is your wife doing?" question with, "We are both having good days and bad days."

I, like a lot of people I think, went back to work as part of my therapy, actively attempting to put my life in perspective and get back into it. In hindsight, I wish I had taken the steps to let people know what I needed. Parents I've spoken with over the years who called their employer or someone they trusted in the workplace before returning to work, had much better experiences than those who didn't. By making that phone call and letting someone know how they were doing and what would be helpful when they came back, the ice was broken and some of the dread of seeing people for the first time was lessened. For the most part, people want to say and do the right thing, but they simply do not know what that is. As for the insensitive people you will inevitably come across, gently remind them how lucky they are to have the good fortune of being ignorant.

Will having another baby make it better?

Sherokee One of the first things I heard from people was, "Have another baby, and it will be better." Getting a new car after a car has been totaled in an accident seems appropriate. Rebuilding a house after a fire makes sense. But getting pregnant again or adopting shortly after our baby—a unique, loved person died—seemed ludicrous!

Isn't it first necessary to honor that person, remember them, and cry or be sad because they are missing from our daily life? Will having another baby really make it all better? Or is this 'quick fix' just an attempt to move someone from pain to joy by avoiding the very process they need which will heal them in time and over time (because of the hard work of mourning, not due only to passage of time). It doesn't seem possible that anyone can really believe that simply having another baby will make us forget this love of our life. Yet, some people do— family, friends and even some parents who are in the 'fix it' or the 'denial' mode. Our babies were, and are, so precious to us that they can never be replaced, and they will live on in our hearts forever. Healing first makes sense, although when we are impatient to have another baby, this does make it hard.

I did find the energy and motivation to teach aerobics again— eight hours a week to get in shape for another pregnancy—and it did make me feel better. Within six months we were pregnant again. The pregnancy was long; each day seemed like a year. We were afraid to be hopeful or talk much about our plans. Yet, I didn't want this baby to sense s/he was unwanted or that we had more fear than love. Sometimes, when I was afraid, I tried to talk with David about it. I kept a journal, and about once a month we went shopping as our hopeful gesture that all would be okay. Feeling afraid that it would happen again bonded us. We couldn't pretend to be blissfully ignorant about what could happen. On the other hand, we wanted to have some normalcy in the pregnancy and wanted a positive attitude. I believe the baby knew our stress and heard our words, so outwardly I acted hopeful, and inside I constantly prayed for a healthy baby. Little changes in the pregnancy and baby's movement scared me, but I didn't always give the details to David, not wanting to scare him, too. I went in to the clinic often for those 'reassurance' checks telling him about them maybe half the time. I was trying to control what little I could in this pregnancy.

When we did finally have Kellan and subsequently, Trevor, we both realized that another baby could not take away our sorrow. Don't get me wrong; it helped a ton. We loved our next sons and quickly became preoccupied with their little lives, which filled us with such love. However, especially in the early weeks and months, they reminded us of who we had been missing—Brenna, Marama, and our smallest baby Bryna (ectopic pregnancy.) Over time, the focus clearly went to parenting our living sons, and we put our other babies more in the background. I tried really hard not to feel like I was being disloyal to them, something many parents have also expressed. I am thankful I had done so much of my grief work, because I believe I was a better, more appreciative, and wise parent.

So be careful of this one. Expecting another pregnancy to be an answer to the tough grief work isn't wise. Know that subsequent children cannot replace their sibling who died. In fact, they may remind you of who is missing and how your lives are less full...and that could backfire if your plan is to seek happiness, not sadness. If one of you insists on another baby right away, do discuss the importance of some healing work first. It is very complicated and challenging to become pregnant soon after a loss. Some experts believe that babies can hear at 14-16 weeks in utero, therefore parents may want to speak positive, hope-filled thoughts. If the fear of bonding and unresolved grief promote negativity, it could be picked up by your next baby. The need to mourn and deal with the missing child before having another baby makes sense for many reasons. Keep talking and sharing your concerns, fears, hopes, and dreams as well. This time can be less stressful if you depend on each other to provide that balance.

Tim Monica became pregnant three months after Kathleen's birth. That meant that the subsequent pregnancy followed the same timeframe as Kathleen's. Of course we were both excited at the prospect of another baby, but our timing probably left a little to be desired.

I believe that Monica, for the most part, was able to concentrate on enjoying every minute she carried the baby inside her. I, on the other hand, spent most of the nine months preparing myself for another loss. In the end, we were ecstatic to have a healthy little boy, but his birth was not a magic pill that suddenly made our sense of loss disappear.

Do not fall into the trap of thinking that another pregnancy will be a cure for your grief. But do not become paralyzed with fear and a sense of doom either. I lived for nine months with a throbbing headache and an emotional tug-of-war...some moments I would be excited we were going to have another child, and the next moment I would try to convince myself that I was prepared for another loss. By protecting myself in that way, I believed it would not hurt as much if it happened again.

Stuck in the muck of sadness and pain

Sherokee With all my focus on my new mission to help other bereaved parents, I think I forgot to find happiness in many moments or at times in my life. I believe that is what David kept trying to tell me over and over again.

Unfortunately, I fought that most of the time. I now believe that we can, in some ways, create our own chaos and unhappiness — or light and hopefulness — through our thoughts and actions. By that I mean, when I was down, I could find reasons to stay there for days. However, when I choose to set those thoughts aside for a little while, I found reasons to smile or laugh, even if but for a few moments. Maybe I welcomed a sunrise or watched a sunset in awe. Or I spent time in my garden smiling because my flowers made me feel better.

Too often in those first six months after Brennan's death I

would not allow happiness in my heart or my day. I was adding to my own discontent by blocking out the pleasure and light. Many parents say that by focusing on the pain and hurt they could stay close to their child. If I could do it over again, I wish I had sought more music (especially to help me sleep at night), poetry, nature, exercise, and even more mealtimes with friends. I wish I had remembered that life is about attitude and that we can take more control. And I wish I had leaned on God more, asking for help to bring more beauty and blessings into our home.

In addition, at the time I did not realize the importance of some laughter, good nutrition, sunlight, sleep, and drinking lots of water. These basics can make all the difference when it comes to healing and getting life back to a sense of normalcy. When I wasn't getting enough sleep, I was cranky and didn't think too well. Not eating or eating too much junk food added to my problems. I wish I had practiced more healthy choices. Maybe my healing would have come sooner, and my daily decisions and interactions with David might have been better.

A body in motion stays in motion. Maybe a body focused on unhappiness and sadness stays in that cycle. Therefore, my suggestion to you is to allow some happiness inside your life, even in the midst of your pain. It doesn't have to be for a full day, but it could be. You get to decide. Try smiling at someone, even if you don't feel it inside. Take a walk or work out, even if it seems like the biggest chore in the world. Sit or work in the sun since vitamin D and limited sun exposure can be helpful in the healing process. Seek ordinary days, let some light shine in, and remember the essentials to good health. You will feel better as a result.

Do these on your own timetable and do them because you want to or feel you should, not because of the pressure from others. Allow yourself some pleasure and it may grow into more pleasure and happiness. Just because you have had such a devastating tragedy doesn't mean you don't deserve or need some beauty and hope in your life. In fact, you do if you are to survive well. This could be helpful for both you and your relationship. Try it. What do you have to lose?

Tim   After months of functioning like I was okay, but never really feeling it, I can recall the period of my grief when I began to realize I could not continue to be cloaked in sadness anymore.

I simply could not continue to feel like I was wearing a heavy-hooded coat that was stopping me from feeling the sun's warmth or seeing what was happening around me. I felt like we were becoming the couple our friends wanted to avoid because we were such downers to be around. I also felt like I couldn't hold a conversation that did not somehow circle back to Kathleen and the sadness that we were living with. I was sick of not having hope and feeling guilty for laughing.

Obviously, my time frame did not miraculously coincide with Monica's emotional state of being. And while I had learned by that point that it probably did not do me any good to pretend she was there with me, it did not stop me from trying to hurry her along. (No one ever accused me of being a fast learner.)

But reaching that fork in the road truly was a turning point for me in my grief. I began to feel that my sadness no longer honored Kathleen. I felt she wanted my memories of her to be happy, and not always accompanied by tears, anger, and a sense of hopelessness. In other words, I was starting to heal.

Does that mean I was never sad again? No. Does that mean I began to forget Kathleen and just focus on the living things around me? Of course not. Does that mean everyone will come to a realization in the way I did? Not a chance.

———————————

This is a critical period for any couple living through grief. It is the time when support from family and friends is starting to wane because they believe you should be moving on. Most likely your employer is expecting you to be back to full productivity (assuming they ever expected you wouldn't be). And often it is when different grieving styles become most obvious, and tolerance for diversity becomes less and less.

You may need to be creative in how you go about communicating during this time. Set a time aside where you each take five minutes to just share how you are doing. Make an agreement that neither of you will say anything while the other is talking. Seek out friends or family members who might be open to talking with you. Find a support group...either locally or online. Change your environment by getting away from the house for awhile, whether it be an evening or a weekend getaway. Don't be afraid to see a grief or marriage counselor. You are not alone in your struggles.

I don't have any words of wisdom that will make this period easy if you find yourselves with divergent coping styles and stuck in the emotion of it all. But I will tell you that patience and understanding are two words you might want to write on the bathroom mirror.

Regrets and guilt

Sherokee While we both knew that communication was the key; some moments we were good at it, other moments not. I couldn't help dwelling on the 'what ifs?' What if I would have gone to the doctor sooner, what if I hadn't danced two nights before, what if some negative thoughts had caused this, what if there was something I had done? Or the worse one, what if God was punishing me for previous sins (we all have them, you know.) There were a few times I could tell David was getting tired of my wallowing and 'active' grieving, and he wanted me to move to the next place sooner.

I now believe that he didn't want me to feel guilty or beat myself up, but that is exactly what I needed to do for awhile. As 'mother protector,' I was supposed to keep my baby safe. And I did not. How do you explain that away? After our third loss (I had a miscarriage first, then Brennan and an ectopic pregnancy after Kellan and Trevor), I remember sitting on the couch with my back to him crying and complaining that I felt like such a failure. He held me, lovingly saying, "You are not a failure, look at our two wonderful boys, Kellan and Trevor." In reply, I pointed out that three out of five pregnancies were failures, the odds were on the failure side. What could he say? I felt responsible. How could he talk me out of that?

Other times, I played games, destructive games, with myself and David. When he came home from work I was sullen and silent. I knew he wouldn't like it, and to a degree I knew he was right; I was dwelling on this a bit too much. I also wanted to see how sensitive David was to my moods and my needs. I didn't feel I should always have to announce my issues and concerns. I wanted him to notice and show he was paying attention. (Remember the "Brain Differences" section above? I had not learned that yet, or I would have realized how painful and destructive this game really was.)

So, I waited for David to bring Brennan's name up. I'd wait and wait but not tell him that I wanted him to broach the subject. Probably he was relieved and hopeful that it might finally be an ordinary night where we talked about life, future, work, or anything but the elephant in the room...Brennan. I would get angry at him for not bringing it up. Obviously, he had moved on and didn't care any longer, I thought. Maybe he didn't even love Brennan as much as I did. Like I said, these were dangerous, destructive games I was playing, which I now regret.

In some ways I was seeking reasons for more pain and holding tight to my anger at the injustice of this loss. I felt guilty for any happy or hopeful feelings. Was this being disloyal to Brennan? I was stuck and didn't know how to get out. Eventually, some fights and arguments began. I never blamed myself, but really I was at fault. It wasn't a glorious time, and it wasn't pretty. I'm thankful we lived through that as a couple. We probably should have sought counseling. Thankfully, we talked things through. Finally, I let go of this destructive behavior. I think I should have prayed more for guidance and help. And it would have helped if I had known then what I know now...

———————————

Make good choices about taking care of your body and your relationship. If you see yourself doing destructive things, stop. If you are religious, pray and seek wisdom and support from clergy. You may also find help from a counselor, a support group, or a wise friend. It is hard to survive when destructive tactics are in use. Your relationship is worth more than this. Work hard right now to move into a different pattern. You both deserve it.

Also be careful of the blame game. Talk it out and try to keep guilt, a normal response, in its proper place. In the end, we did what we did; it happened, and there was now nothing that could be changed. Work on forgiving, letting go, and moving through this as much as you can. Get those feelings out so they don't fester and cause more problems over time.

Tim   I have used the word guilt frequently in what I have written in this book. But I, like many others in our society, have a tendency to misuse it. By its very definition, guilt implies intentional criminal behavior. Yet, we find ourselves feeling 'guilty' because our baby died or how we handled our subsequent grief. While it may not change the actual emotions we are experiencing, a better word might be 'regret'. It is less harsh and more accurately defines the situation.

Almost from the moment I found out that Kathleen had died, I had regrets. Why hadn't I been more excited about the pregnancy and doing all the same 'new dad' things I did when we were expecting our first child? Why had I been so overwhelmed with the thought of saying goodbye to her that I hurried what little time we had? How could I have been so insensitive as to not know how Monica would react when I took down the crib on the first day home? I even worried that maybe some of those unbecoming activities I took part in while in college messed me up more than I thought (even if I didn't inhale.) My initial regrets about what kind of dad I was were quickly followed by feelings of inadequacy as a husband. Why didn't I instinctively know what Monica needed from me? How could I be such a jerk as to cry all the way home from work, but then turn around and give Monica a hard time for being sad? The list could go on and on.

But finally, as the pain started to diminish and I was able to put things in perspective, I was better able to understand that most of us would live our lives differently if we knew what tragedy was waiting to ambush us around the next bend. I attempted to take the time to learn how to truly value and cherish my life and family, and I tried to let go of the past, knowing that it was impossible to rewrite.

In the final analysis, there was no doubt that Kathleen was a child whom Monica and I both wanted. We tried to be good parents from the moment we found out we were expecting her, and there was zero doubt in either of our minds as to how much she was loved.

Regardless of what we call it, guilt or regret can be a destructive emotion if taken to extremes. While I think Sherokee is correct in saying that sometimes we may need to feel guilty (have regrets) for awhile after a significant loss, try to keep it in perspective.

And, when interacting with your partner, be especially cautious of innocent comments that can be interpreted as laying blame. One of my most vivid memories of the early days after Kathleen died, is when Monica innocently asked me if I felt guilty for not being more involved in the pregnancy – doing things like talking to her stomach and sleeping with my hand on her belly so I could feel the baby's movements. Because I truly was feeling guilty about those things – even though I hadn't verbalized it – stabbing me in the heart would have likely been less painful than having her ask that question. I recall wondering if I could ever forgive her, or whether our marriage had ended at that moment. Luckily, she quickly realized she had struck a nerve and explained that she was asking out of concern for me, not in an attempt to accuse me. I have sometimes wondered what might have happened had she not been aware of how hurtful that comment was for me, even though it was honestly not intended in any way to be accusatory.

So, be aware that you are both likely to be highly sensitive during this period, and try to get clarification before jumping to conclusions — whether it be in regard to perceived behaviors or spoken words.

Escaping – dependency on drugs, alcohol, or other methods

Sherokee I do think I escaped when I stayed up quite late to write or when I slept in. My intensity and full time passion for this endeavor allowed me to escape the other parts of life — like cooking, cleaning up, going back to my previous work and school, and even putting quality time into our relationship. In retrospect, I am ever grateful to David. Mostly he didn't interfere with what I needed to do. I was able to finish the book and move on to my/our new ministry helping bereaved families. So for me, the 'escape thing' worked out pretty well in the end. However, I know of too many partners who left the relationship or escaped the pain with alcohol or drugs. This is very serious and needs to be dealt with.

I noticed that David also found his ways to escape. He spent lots of time outside running long distances, working outdoors, or chopping wood. Those seemed productive to me, though his hunting bugged me. However, when he came home from a hard day at work and turned on the television, I went crazy...I never turned on the television during the day and hardly at night. It seemed a waste of time. He would stare at it but did not appear to be 'into' the program. When I asked him what he was watching, he would often respond, "Oh, I don't know. Nothing really." Now it even seemed more of a waste. What was the point? I wondered. Later on I read the book, *Men are from Mars, Women are from Venus* and I realized what was going on. In the old 'caveman' days, men sat in front of the fire, relaxing and releasing the stress of the day. Nowadays, the fire isn't as accessible to most men, but television is. It has become the new 'fire' for some. While the television de-stress strategy still drives me a bit crazy, at least I understand the reason for it and am somewhat (notice I say somewhat) more accepting. And in the scheme of life, it is much better than turning to drugs or alcohol.

The need to escape is real. The methods you choose are important. Seek productive or less harmful choices. If you do find yourself choosing destructive means to escape such as drinking or using drugs, talk with someone. You are not only hurting yourself, but your partner as well. This is a set up for dangerous behaviors that could put your relationship in jeopardy. Mike, a recently bereaved father, stated that after escaping with alcohol for awhile, he found the courage to listen to his wife and face his loss. By doing that, he felt content they would survive.

Tim I have already talked about my escape to the lawnmower and finding relief from my sadness by being busy at work or driving alone in the car. Thank goodness I was at a spot in my life at the time where I did not see alcohol or many other potentially destructive behaviors as an option. I simply did not have time to consider such things.

In the years since, however, I have periodically caught myself looking forward to a drink at the end of the day when I am particularly stressed about something. While I don't feel that drinking is necessarily a horrible thing, red flags start going up when my motivation is to try and numb what is bothering me. I have also struggled with escaping to the internet when trying to distract myself from life's pressures.

Just keep in mind that it is very easy to justify any seemingly benign behavior that is done in moderation, but the real trick is distinguishing between what is moderate and what is excessive. After all, who can't rationalize a beer now and then or the need to do 'research' on the web? Certainly one gauge is that if you later feel guilty for your behavior, it probably is an indication that you are engaging in activities that you wouldn't normally do, and you should look long and hard at what potential impact it could have on you and your family.

Some partners, often fathers, overwork or play extra hard as a way of coping with their pain. In the Grief Recovery class I teach, we refer to these behaviors as STERBS — Short Term Energy Relieving Behaviors. STERBS are a way for us to release the stockpiled emotions that amass if we don't give our grief a voice. We become like the proverbial teapot that blows its lid if there is no way to discharge the steam.

One of the most tragic stories I ever heard from a grieving dad was from a man who lost everything after the death of his child. He shared that he refused to talk about his feelings with his wife, getting angry if she tried to push him into communicating. He quickly buried himself in his work in the weeks following the death, and soon his Friday beer night with the guys became Monday through Friday beer nights with the guys. He was gone so much that he missed his living children's evening activities and became a stranger to them. One Friday night he came home from the bar to discover his family was gone, with a note saying that his wife did not love him anymore and that he should be out of the house by Monday morning. That week he started counseling. As this man shared his story, most of us in the room were waiting for the part where he said that his family's departure brought him to his knees, and he finally got the help he needed and saved his marriage. Sadly, he went through his recovery process alone.

If going home at night seems to be too stressful and talking does not feel like a viable coping strategy, be careful, and try to realize that this behavior can become dangerous to your health and to your relationship. If you shut your partner out for an extended time, it is likely you will not have to ignore them for long. They'll be gone. So, chop wood, work on cars, mow the grass, exercise, read, write...but do make time to go home. You need each other now more than ever.

Be very careful about abusive behaviors. They will only make things worse for you personally and can damage your relationship. Seek help from a clergy, support group, or counselor. If you feel depressed, talk with someone about it right away. This is especially imperative if you really feel you want to hurt someone or die and find yourself thinking of how that could be accomplished. Call someone immediately if you can relate to any of these behaviors.

Spirituality, faith, and forgiveness

Sherokee We did not have a church family due to a recent move and the fact that we were still struggling with spirituality and religion—how to incorporate it into our lives.

When Brennan died, we realized that without faith in God we were not going to make it. So we prayed and tried to integrate God into our lives more. Struggling with God's role in the death was constant for both of us. Did He cause it? Did He allow it? What were we to learn from it, and more importantly what were we to do because of it? At times we were angry with Him. Then at times we thought that He too had lived through the death of his son and surely wouldn't purposely make others go through that. We read books about God and found *Why Do Bad Things Happen to Good People* by Rabbi Kuschner, which helped us immensely.

Empty Arms was finished in about nine months after Brennan's death. Once completed, I realized that God had worked through me. How could I have possibly had such wisdom while in the middle of such pain and self-centeredness? I am now thankful that we were open to faith and God. Visiting churches became important to us. Sadly, we did not turn to the Bible, which in retrospect might have helped us more than anything. That is a regret I still have.

The slowly evolving concept of forgiveness challenged me over the years. I didn't find anger productive, and I believe I hurt myself and my relationship with people by holding onto that anger. In time, I came to understand...and practice when I could...that forgiveness was an amazing gift I could give myself and the people with whom I was upset (friends who avoided me after the losses, people who said hurtful things, the staff for not taking pictures and doing a better job of helping us receive mementos, David and myself for making bad decisions, etc, etc, etc). I prayed for wisdom and strength to forgive and sometimes even wrote to people apologizing for my behaviors and asking them to forgive me. That was the ultimate in difficulty, but boy did I sleep well after doing that a few times. I felt a weight lifted off my shoulders and my heart each time I was able to let go and forgive. Now if I could just forgive myself more often, I'd feel I have this 'forgiveness thing' somewhat under control.

Some people turn away from God at this time. They cannot rationalize how a loving God could allow such a horrible thing to happen. This could be the very time they probably need to be carried by God. If you find yourself angry at God, know that you are not alone. Seek support from others and keep the channels open if you can. It is my belief that God knows your pain and will help. We just can't always know when and how that help will come.

Tim As I shared earlier, our priest did not feel that our loss warranted any type of response, including a hospital visit or memorial service. I am quite confident that the lack of support we witnessed was unique, but the failure of this one person to take action greatly impacted how we perceived God, the church, and even our most fundamental beliefs. While a part of me certainly understood that the failings of this man were human errors, he still represented the organized church, and I was already angry with God for letting Kathleen die. Given our raw pain at the time, bitterness and anger quickly became by-products, and an already difficult situation became hurtful. In hindsight, maybe it was not all bad that we had a place to focus our anger, because it prevented us from venting those feelings on each other.

It's been many years, but I still find myself tense whenever I drive by that daunting church structure that so coldly represents those moments of my life. While for us it was easy to be disappointed in those humans who represented our faith, I found it hard to remain angry with God for too long. While I questioned whether Kathleen's death was punishment for my not being more involved in her pregnancy or for taking for granted that my children would be healthy and happy, the deepest parts of who I am knew that God didn't work that way. I couldn't believe in a God who would hurt my child because of my personal failings, and I eventually found myself praying in my private way, asking for help in moving on and feeling happiness once more.

It was not, however, until I was being trained as a Grief Recovery® Specialist that I really thought about my need to forgive and, more importantly, what that meant. The training facilitator pointed out that forgiveness is not an emotion, it's an action. Beyond that, it is often an action that needs to occur before it can truly be felt. It seems we frequently confuse 'forgiveness' with 'condoning,' and that is where we get hung up. By forgiving someone for what they did or failed to do, you are not saying that it was okay, but rather, that *you* are not going to let it hurt *you* anymore. In other words, forgiveness is about you, and it's in your control whether you choose to take that action. In the Grief Recovery® course, we say that forgiveness is 'giving up the hope for a different or better yesterday.' If you really think about that, you may well find yourself feeling empowered rather than an angry victim.

———————————

When an event out of the natural order of life occurs, like a baby dying, it is not unusual for some to be angry with God. If you find yourself being in that position, don't beat yourself up. But also know that isolating yourself from beliefs that may have brought you strength up until this point in your life can make your grief feel that much more lonely and confusing. Be open to share your feelings with your clergy or other people you respect. The very act of expressing your anger and disappointment will help you heal. If, on the other hand, you are able to find comfort in knowing that your child is with God, be grateful for that gift.

Compromise and getting along

Sherokee While I believe doing our own thing worked for some of the time, we did need to intersect in our process at least occasionally. I needed to give in some to David and vice versa. We kept each other in balance much of the time, and we made time to talk with each other. When I had been dwelling too much and not living life, David let me know. I rarely admitted (to him) that he was right, but I did think about what he was saying and sometimes altered what I was doing. I guess I needed to hear that, because I can go off on a tangent convinced that the way I am coping is the only way it can be done. I can also be stubborn, which might have been helpful in some way to my survival but surely made it difficult for David and our relationship. I did go out more than I wanted to and tried to be sociable even when I found it hard.

Compromise helped me keep things in perspective...at least some of the time. I asked David to face things—his feelings, our changed journey—more than he wished. As much as he didn't want to go there with me often enough from my perspective, mostly he did out of love for me and for Brennan. I appreciate that. How hard it must have been for him, yet out of it came some good things.

Seek compromise whenever you can if it seems doable and right. Listen to each other and as time goes on attempt to gain some perspective on this tunnel of pain you are in.

Tim For the most part, I don't recall needing to compromise any more after Kathleen's death than before. As a matter of fact, in the early weeks, I think we were both raw enough and needed each other's support so much that neither of us rocked the boat too much.

The most vivid memories I have of compromise came on two occasions. The first was when we were trying to decide whether to go to a support group. For me, it was not a question to discuss. I wasn't going. When it became clear that Monica was going to go with or without me, my adopted Catholic guilt took hold and I couldn't stand the thought of her going alone, so I pouted as we drove to the hospital and nearly passed out from fear when I entered that room for the first time.

The next real compromise came on Kathleen's first birthday. Monica wanted to take the day off work and spend it together, starting off by attending morning mass. My vote was to either stay in bed with a pillow over my head or bury myself so deep in work that I would not have time to breathe, much less think. Needless to say, guilt reared its ugly head once more and I went to church. It was a good experience, and, after that, Monica was content to spend some time alone while I worked part of the day. That night we had a little party and Emily blew out the candle on Kathleen's cake, ending the day on a hopeful note that would never have occurred if left to me.

Compromise is an essential ingredient in any relationship – whether with your mate, your business partner, or the co-author of a book you are writing! During extremely stressful times, when you might be feeling particularly vulnerable and/or insecure anyway, finding the middle ground can be tough. Keep in mind that you are both likely experiencing emotions you have not had before, especially as a couple, and neither of you has any clear answers as to what is right or wrong.

Much time has passed

Sherokee How do we sum up for you twenty-five years of coping, arguing, remembering, growing, and loving? For years now, we have more smiles than tears when we talk of our heavenly babies. Thankfully, we had a rather solid relationship before our losses. No doubt that helped. Working through such tension and pain was not easy; at times it was downright brutal. However, we had decided not to give up on each other. We wanted our marriage to work, and we desperately wanted to have a family. Sometimes we ignored the pain and acted normal. That helped. Sometimes we dwelled on it, and that helped. We prayed often for patience and reminders that we needed each other, and that we had committed our future to each other. Surely, that helped. No relationship is perfect; ours was far from flawless. But we have managed to stay married, most of it quite happily, for over 30 years. For that we are thankful.

And we are hopeful for you. Remind yourself why you chose each other and what you wish to yet achieve. Find reasons to make it work, then take steps toward that goal. Love each other fully, and keep talking. Give in and compromise when you can, and then do more. Keep your thoughts positive, and be good to yourself. Seek outside help before you are feeling too desperate. Use your resources and your humor appropriately. Believe you can make it, and believe in each other. Above all else, remember your love for each other and your baby.

Tim It is really quite amazing to me that I can still so vividly recall the hours and days surrounding Kathleen's birth. And while the pain associated with those memories is much less intense than it once was, it still exists. I think that one of the ways to help dull the sadness over the years is to take the time to reflect on what you have learned, and be grateful for the positive moments that came about as a result of this experience.

We established a tradition on Kathleen's first birthday of going to the tree we planted in her memory, releasing balloons, and then going out to dinner. That ritual is still going strong 25 years later, even though the party format continues to evolve. I was always proud of the fact that our four living children never questioned keeping that custom alive, even when in high school playing sports, juggling boyfriends and girl-friends, or keeping up with homework. There is something very symbolic of the love that lives on in all our hearts when seeing your teenage football player standing in a public park holding a pink balloon, oblivious to the stares he garners from passersby.

I share that story not only because it represents a tradition that has lasted so many years, but because it also demonstrates the positive moments that can result from the hard work of com-municating, compromising, and searching for the desire to live again. As I talked about earlier, my initial instincts in life had always been to stay in my comfort zone. I rarely stepped out-side the box and made myself vulnerable to others, especially Monica. In the moments after Kathleen's death, my emotional walls collapsed and I could no longer keep my tears private. When 'forced' to attend a support group, I learned that I was not the only male to face these fears, and the weight of trying to hold everything inside began to lift. The birthday tradition I shared above would not exist if I had not been open to trusting Monica's instincts for creating memories for our children who were yet to be born. She understood that importance. I didn't.

I could find many more examples of the gifts that Kathleen's short life brought my own, not the least of which are the friends like Sherokee and David who came into our lives as a result. Unless you happen to write a book or in some other way are forced to reflect on your life since your baby's death, you could easily miss the opportunity to recognize these bright spots in an otherwise dark period of your life. I can tell you they are worth searching for, because they both honor your baby and offer the gift healing.

If you are reading this book, most likely you have had a relatively recent loss. We hope that as your pain eases, you find appropriate ways to give your grief a voice and move forward. It is then that you will be able to truly realize all the wonderful gifts this baby has brought you and those you know. You will likely touch people in your lives in a way that you would not have otherwise. And, hopefully, you will look back at this time as one of healing together and strengthening your bond with your partner. While not one of us would ever choose to be taught these lessons, with hard work and lots of compromise, your relationship can be richer for having lived through this experience.

Other couples' differing perspectives

Delaying grief work until our partner is better...

Rhoda and Tom For the most part of a year, Rhoda grieved as many women do—boldly, emotionally, and constantly. She was giving back to other bereaved parents through her volunteer efforts. She was also desperately seeking understanding and some emotion from her husband. But it just did not seem to come anymore after the first few weeks or so. She feared he did not care anymore and wondered how he could be so calm working every day and not seeming to be 'bothered' by the emptiness and sorrow that was in her life. Around a year after the death, it was clear that Rhoda was healing and finding some happiness again. She had a bounce in her step and did not dwell on her baby's death like before. Suddenly, it seemed, Tom became despondent and was even to be found secretly crying. When they finally talked about it, Tom told Rhoda that now he knew she was safe and feeling better he could let his feelings out. This surprised Rhoda, but is actually fairly common with the 'protector' type partner. For all that time he had been her rock, her support, and he put his grief work on hold. Then it hit him, once he knew his partner was better. His baby died, too, and he needed *his* time to allow the feelings to come forward. Of course, the problem was complicated for him since it was a year later and few were there for him in his grief.

The decisions made in the early days following the loss...

Ryan and Sandra Not only can the decisions that you make come back to haunt you, but so can the decisions that you don't make. While in the hospital awaiting the birth of Porter Ann, the nurses asked us if we wanted to hold her. Both Sandra and I really had a difficult time with this decision. Sandra's first reaction was to distance herself as much as possible from her dead child. She didn't want to see her or hold her, she just wanted to concentrate on the task at hand and make it through her birth.

I, on the other hand, knew that I wanted to see my daughter and hold her. I knew that I needed to say hello and goodbye. But I also knew that Sandra was having a hard time with the thought of this. I asked Sandra to reconsider since this was her daughter and she should hold her. Sandra eventually agreed and did indeed see her and hold her.

When Porter Ann was born and the nurses brought her to us, Sandra held our daughter for just a few moments before being overwhelmed with emotions. I then took Porter Ann and held her in my own arms for the remainder of the time that we spent with her. I remember thinking at the time that Sandra should be holding her, but I tried to protect her because she was having such a difficult time with things.

Both Sandra and I are so incredibly thankful to this day that I was able to convince her to reconsider her original position and that she did get the chance to see and hold Porter Ann. But now I'm left with this incredible guilt inside for holding Porter Ann longer and not asking if Sandra wanted to hold her again. I can only imagine the guilt I would feel now if I had never convinced Sandra to begin with and she never had the chance to hold her daughter at all.

Making assumptions is NOT communication...

No matter how well you think you know your partner, you still cannot read their minds and know what they are thinking. When in doubt, communication and asking each other what you are thinking and feeling is the only sure way to under-stand each other. Emotions, feelings, and state of mind can change from one moment to the next during the grieving process, and a couple's reaction to these changing emotions can vary drastically as well.

On one particular occasion, I remember waking up one day feeling rather depressed and sad, more so than usual, as this was one of those particularly bad days. I have a tendency to withdraw and keep to myself when I feel really sad and depressed. Sandra didn't understand this new and suddenly drastic change in my demeanor and took it as a sign that I must have been upset with her. She, in return, decided to give me some space in an attempt to not upset me further. She also felt frustrated with me since she misinterpreted my depression as anger towards her, so her reaction to this was to withdraw from me and basically give me the 'silent treatment.'

This was the opposite of what I needed at that point in time. While I was quite sad and depressed and didn't feel the energy to reach out to Sandra, I so desperately needed her to reach out to me and give me support during this difficult day. Instead, I spent the day with no support and only questions racing through my head as to why I was getting the cold shoulder from Sandra. After an entire day at work not talking to one another (the first day without talking since Porter Ann died), I finally couldn't take it anymore and confronted Sandra about what was wrong. We soon found out that nothing was wrong other than our own misguided assumptions for what the other was feeling.

We agreed from that day forward that we would never try to 'perceive' what the other was feeling, and would instead keep an open dialog as to avoid further misunderstandings.

Spirituality and faith...

Sometimes acceptance of God and religion takes time. Sandra and I know that spirituality and faith in God can help us through this. We want to feel close to God so that we can in turn feel closer to Porter Ann. But unfortunately that is easier said than done. We still question God for taking Porter Ann from us. We are angry with God and question our faith. I think that this is just a phase or process that we must go through before being able to accept God and Porter Ann's death. About three weeks after Porter Ann died, we thought that we would attend church. Maybe it would help us heal and make us feel closer to Porter. Unfortunately, we had a pretty hard time dealing with church and God that day. Maybe it was too soon; maybe Porters death and our pain were too fresh. It's now been two months and we haven't returned. We hope one day to be able to make it past these feelings and once again embrace God and our faith, but right now we just aren't ready.

Feeling vulnerable and fearful...

We can relate to fear of the death of other children we hope to have someday, in that we feared for the death of our spouse. Both Sandra and I remember not wanting to let each other out of our sight, fearing the worst. We had horrible worries that the other would die from a car wreck or some other horrible accident. I think we just felt so vulnerable during those early days and weeks that we realized we just couldn't handle another loss. We also had this uncontrollable fear when it came to our dog. Before Porter Ann died we would often let our dog out in our front yard or walk without a leash. We could even run inside briefly and leave him out there without worry as he always stuck by our side and never wandered off. But after Porter Ann died, we started watching him like a hawk. We had an uncontrollable fear that he would run out into the road and get hit by a car. Again, I think this overprotection was just a defense mechanism because we realized that we couldn't handle another loss.

Coping differently...

Sandra's family background and way of dealing with feelings surrounding a loss differed quite dramatically from mine. Sandra was brought up to push away the feelings and to not talk about them. When Porter Ann died, Sandra's family tried to take her mind off of losing our daughter by not talking about Porter and by distancing themselves from her. When her family called, they avoided the topic of Porter Ann and tried to keep the conversation light and upbeat.

My family was quite the opposite. I was brought up to confront grief head on as I was taught that the grieving process should be shared very openly with family members and even counselors if needed. Thus, my family called almost daily through the first few months and talked sometimes for hours about Porter Ann and the feelings and emotions surrounding her death.

Because of the family support that I received, I could share things outside of my relationship with Sandra. Although we had different feelings, different emotions, and different ways of dealing with things, we were in fact both grieving the same thing – the loss of our daughter. I found it very helpful to find solace and comfort with others. It was as if I could get an out-side perspective or simply have another shoulder to cry on.

Sandra, on the other hand, didn't have this outlet. She was raised to hold her feelings inside. Therefore, she only had me to talk with and seek comfort from.

After about four weeks it was apparent that this just simply wasn't working. Sandra had reached her breaking point. She had a meltdown and simply couldn't stop crying. Her grief was bottled up inside too long, and she needed someone else to talk with besides her husband.

So, she called her family and just started opening up to them and sharing her grief with them. She also started talking with friends and co-workers. This gave her another outlet, another shoulder to cry on, or just another person to hug. As a couple, we must realize that we can't get everything that we need simply from one another and that we must also look to our friends and family for additional support.

Back to work, back to life...

Sometimes normalcy is forced on you and not really desired. Unfortunately, sometimes you can't just withdraw from your life and shut yourself inside to grieve. If I had this option I would have done it, but bills still have to be paid and I couldn't just quit my job. So, reluctantly I re-entered my life after taking a few weeks off to be with Sandra and grieve for Porter Ann. This was very tough to do. The first few weeks were extremely unproductive as I found myself staring blankly into the computer or out the window and didn't get much of any work done; I was constantly thinking about Porter. Then after a little while back, I had to start getting into the regular tasks of my job, and it seemed that I was starting to get back to my normal routine. This was very hard to deal with since I hated being preoccupied with anything other than sitting around thinking about Porter.

Coping Differently...

Wendy and Tom Wendy shared a perspective that better explained the differences in grieving. In her family, when there was pain it was viewed as an infection that needed to be drained (talked about and dealt with openly). Thus, after her baby died she was constantly 'draining' the wound. However, her husband and his family believed that wounds got infected and caused more pain over time if they were touched and 'picked at.' They preferred to leave the scab alone believing it would heal by itself. Therefore, he preferred not talking about the baby after a few weeks and didn't 'pick' at the pain. Rather, through silence and by moving on, he was helping it to heal. Different approaches to the same loss. One did not love their baby less, but they each had their own view on how to heal.

Accept your loss...

Susan Erling Martinez   I divorced years after my still-birth, so I have a different perspective than Tim and Sherokee. On average, close to half of all couples do eventually divorce, especially after the stress of hardship. But I believe these 'big happenings' in life are in a way predestined. I believe they arrive at our doorsteps to change us for the better. Accept that this experience is an integral piece of the 'big picture' of a person's life. My point: Try to see the bigger picture of your life. Try to see how this experience is vitally important to your growth and betterment as a person and hopefully as a couple.

Forgiveness...

Pat   The hardest person of all to forgive is yourself. I am always telling grieving moms to, "Be kind to yourself." In essence, I ask them to forgive themselves for what they perceive they might have done wrong, for not seeing their mate's grief, and for not understanding their own. It is also important that they forgive themselves for how they react to others, as well as forgive others who are also grieving. Relatives may become distant or seem uncaring because they feel robbed of ever getting to know the baby or because they donít know how to help the bereaved through their tragedy. I often say that through this process, some friends may become strangers, and some strangers may become friends. If we reversed roles, we ourselves might say and do the wrong things. It is only because of our experience that we have learned what the wrong things ever are. Forgiveness is important in the grieving and healing process.

It is what it is...

Steve and Charmayne   My whole world changed when I found out that my baby's heart had stopped beating. Bryce was delivered on October 9th— 9lbs., 6oz and 22 inches long, He was beautiful, big, and absolutely perfect! During delivery I went into what I call 'survival mode'— "I can do this," was all I kept telling myself. Once I could hold him, and cry for the loss of this beautiful baby boy, I again retreated into survival mode. I had a funeral to plan and things to do, again that little voice, "You can do this!" We planned the most beautiful memorial service I have ever attended, and we all made it through. Then the fear set in, now what would happen? All the planning was done, and the event was over. Now what? Survival mode went out the window, and it was time to feel all the horrible emotions that I had been holding at bay. Each day I got up and sent my 10 and 8-year-olds off to school, waited for their bus to leave, and then fell apart. Usually this cry lasted about an hour or longer depending on which memory made me cry. Initially, I was reliving the whole two days and knowing that Bryce was gone, yet I still had to deliver him, then the delivery itself, and then the emptiness of my arms!

I decided to help myself. I found Sherokee Ilse's book *Empty Arms* and read the book cover to cover crying the whole way through; her words inspired me. I'M NOT ALONE, were the words that kept coming to mind. It really felt like Sherokee was sitting beside me and talking to me and telling me I was not alone, and I would be okay. I am so very grateful for the impact her words had in my life.

Once I passed the 2nd month milestone and cried myself hoarse, I decided that the only way I was going to make it through this tragedy was to take a step back, put my broken heart on hold (for a moment), and let my head talk. I am a big believer in your heart has no brains, just emotion, so look at this tragedy with your brain not just your heart!!

It was at this point that I realized that there is absolutely nothing that I could do about losing Bryce. He is my baby that just was never meant to be! Crying was not going to change any of this! Feeling sorry for myself, was not going to change it! I had two children who needed their mom, who needed me to be me, not the empty shell who lost their baby brother. So from that point on I told myself, "There is nothing that I can do to change any of the events that have happened. For whatever reason, Bryce was not meant to live with my family. I must accept all of this for what it is — the biggest tragedy that I have ever experienced!! I must start picking up the pieces of my life and live them. *It is what it is!* Nothing is going to change it. So, accept it, Charmayne, and move forward!!"

Steve and I were grieving very differently and up until recently, seemingly very alone. Not that long ago, we had a major misunderstanding that turned into a full-fledged argument which resulted in us not speaking for about a day. I finally approached him and asked if are we were going to talk about this. I was not ready to give up on us and this marriage of 14 years just because we disagreed. We talked and cried for hours. I found out that things that don't affect my day to day living, consume his. For example, Steve's drive to and from work is just over an hour and he is having a really hard time during this time with too much time to think about what should have been. I told him my, "It is what it is," theory and he said that since that talk those words have helped him. The drive may be long, but he doesn't dwell on what should have been or what could have been. Instead, he just remembers what it was like to hold our son and how beautiful he was and forever will be. And now the lines of communication are more open than before; Steve still does not want to talk about our tragedy at any great length, but he does want to remember all the love we both have for Bryce, and use it in a positive light, for both of us and our family.

I still have bad moments, not days, but moments. I call it the 'emotion wave.' When it hits, I ride it out and then continue with whatever I was doing. It is my choice to not let the 'emotion wave' consume me. I don't think that my precious baby Bryce would want me to not live or to not care for his siblings and his daddy, but most of all I am sure that Bryce would not want me to give up being *me*!

Although Sherokee and I have grieved very differently, her words continue to inspire me and let me know that it's okay to feel the way that I do, and that I don't have to grieve the same way she did. We are all unique individuals! My heart will always have a piece of it missing, but the part of it that's currently broken will heal. My beautiful baby Bryce will always and forever live in my heart and in my mind; it is *here* that I have to keep real so that his place in me will always be okay. *It is what it is!*

(Some names have been changed to maintain confidentiality.)

In conclusion

Sherokee Writing this book has reminded me of the intense pain and energy it took to survive. Though exhausting, the hard work was worth it. There were no books to guide us, so we stumbled often and actually did well at other times. Few support groups existed and the web was not even an option for years after our loss. Thankfully, that has changed and you need not feel as alone as we 'pioneers' felt if you will seek out the resources and people who are waiting to help.

I have wishes; I have regrets. Maybe by sharing them with you, you might learn from them. Or maybe not. It just depends if you are able to learn from others' mistakes/advice or if you are one who learns best from experiencing it yourself. I wish I had been more aware of David's true feelings—I might have given him more of a break. I wish I would have been a better listener and shared what I needed more openly and more often. Daring to give voice to my thoughts and desires meant taking responsibility for them; I was such a novice at this 'grief' thing that I feared everything I wanted to do or say was probably wrong. I questioned my instincts constantly. As I have already mentioned, I also did not seek enough light and sunshine in my days. In being too serious and focused, I missed opportunities to smile and see life's beauty, not only its pain.

Despite it all, I am grateful we weathered the storm and that we often found places and times to agree and to disagree. I am also grateful that David was so patient and loving with me. Sometimes, I fear I was less so with him.

In closing, again I say, trust your instincts. Be open and honest. Expect to grieve and live differently from now on. If you are more in line with each other's grief needs, consider that a beautiful gift. Tell your partner what you need when you need it. Expect to compromise sometimes and not always get what you want. Find others to give you support. When your partner says or does something that seems to hurt you or bothers you, first of all check to see if your perception is the same as what s/he meant. It could be miscommunication or misinterpretation. Believe you will make it, and grow from this. Your attitude will make such a difference. Finally, believe the best in each other, not the worst. Give each other the benefit of the doubt as often as you can.

Tim   When Sherokee and I first decided to work on this project, we had numerous discussions about what we felt should be included in the book before writing our final outline. Following that, Sherokee, being the go-getter of this duo, dug in first to write what she had to share. When she was done, she sent me the manuscript so I could do my part. As I was sitting at the computer trying to meet my deadline, I felt myself getting frustrated with her for adding new sections without telling me (that's my side of it) and seemingly 'talking too much.' And when I complained, she pushed me to write about the topics I had not agreed to cover. Begrudgingly, I usually obliged. Later on, she had a tendency to send me the 'edited' manuscript in Microsoft Word, looking for my review and input. Somehow, in my sections, blue highlighted phrases and paragraphs I had no recollection of writing, miraculously appeared—usually with a little note saying,

"Tim, I think you forgot to put this in." Yeah, right.

Then it hit me. Maybe the experience of putting this book together created more of the dynamic of a couple communicating than either of us anticipated it would!

But seriously, what it does point to is the fact that trying to find a balance in communication is difficult in any relationship — whether a couple or not. And, realistically, the more essential that communication is, the more effort it takes to search for a compromise.

Life has dealt your partnership a blow that you did not see coming, nor one you deserve. But the bottom line is — you are the only two people who can make your relationship survive and grow from this experience. That knowledge can be both frightening and empowering at the same time. The key may be in learning to not only give your own grief a voice, but allowing for the fact that your partner's voice is not merely an echo of your own.

My final suggestion to you is this — when the going gets tough, ask yourselves what your child, whom you conceived in love, would want for you? Then the answer can be seen more clearly, and the hard work it takes to make it happen seems more worthwhile.

Daddy's Grieve Too

It must be so hard on you to be a Dad who grieves,
When real men don't cry or become upset,
Only women do, you are told to believe.

Your dreams are gone,
Your future has changed,
Your wife is just not the same.
You hold your head as high as you can
And play your part of the game.

Your heart just tells you differently,
It aches and hurts you so.
When will someone give you permission,
To let your emotions show?

They ask you how your wife is,
Ignoring the fact you hurt, too.
You answer the question but always wonder
When they will ask about you.

Keep the memory alive of the child you love,
And your love will always shine through.
And maybe one day this world will know
That Daddies always grieve, too.

From Sands TAS June 2001 (SANDS, Queensland)

SHEROKEE ILSE AND TIM NELSON

Love Brings Hope and Life

It begins with love

Wanting more, waiting for new life,
Planning for a future forever changed with
Children.

Then lightening strikes,
Followed by a deep, lonely
Darkness.

Who could be prepared
For this type of anguish?
So alone, yet trying to be
Together.

Love pulls us through
Each day as we struggle to
Survive.

Head down, heart down,
Stress and confusion
Lead to arguments, silence, and
Pain.

Glimpses of beauty
And love eventually bring
Hope.

Life and time
March on, while memories remain.
We are one; we will remember.
Love reminds us to
Live —
Again.

Sherokee Ilse, 2008

Notes and reflections

Questions to prompt conversation

Do you think you understand how your partner is feeling? Do you know what his/her needs are?

After each of you answer these questions, compare notes. It is possible you have held incorrect or misleading perceptions of each other—

In the days following your loss:

How did you perceive your partner acting?

_____

_____

_____

What did you think your partner was feeling emotionally?

_____

_____

_____

What was your perception of how you acted?

_____

_____

_____

What were you experiencing/feeling? Do you think your behavior represented what you were really feeling?

_____

_____

_____

What about today? How are you feeling?

Do you think that you might be holding something against your partner? What is it? Can you talk about it together now?

_____

_____

_____

If you could do something over, what might it be? Share this with your partner; it might help.

_____

_____

_____

Is there something you want to do or need going forward? Share this with your partner; it also might help.

_____

_____

_____

Use the space below to write down other concerns you have.

_____

_____

_____

Couple communication

I am who I am because of where I come from...

Previous life experiences, beliefs, and attitudes can influence you today. Think about the following from the perspective of your youth. While growing up I learned...

It's okay for boys to...

_____

_____

It's not okay for boys to...

_____

_____

It's okay for girls to...

_____

_____

It's not okay for girls to...

_____

_____

How did those beliefs affect how you handled your baby's death at the time and over time?

_____

_____

When I'm upset, stressed out, or in a crisis, I often ...

Feel _____

_____

Need _____

_____

Do _____

_____

To feel better and be comforted, I need and/or do...

_____

_____

_____

Two issues/concerns I am facing now...

1. _____

_____

2. _____

_____

I'd like to say to my partner:

I wish _____

_____

I'm grateful/glad/thankful for _____

_____

To be fixed or not fixed, that is the question.

My feelings about wanting to be fixed by my partner are...

_____

_____

My feelings about being a 'fixer' are...

_____

_____

If I could change one thing about myself, it would be...

_____

_____

If I could change one thing about my partner, it would be...

_____

_____

Emotions—His and Hers

Anguish, sadness, guilt, blame, shame, confusion, anger, exhaustion, fear, regret...

Either on separate pieces of paper or in the lines below, choose some of the emotions you have been feeling and ones that you think your partner has been feeling. Explain why you think you/she/he feels this way, who it might be directed at, etc.

For instance, anger—

I am angry with the doctor, my clergy, and/or myself for

_____

_____

or "I can't feel anger yet. I am too afraid it will _____

_____ ."

or "Sometimes I am so angry with _____

that I _____!

Your turn—

_____

_____

_____

_____

_____

After reading this book and talking with my partner, I have learned the following:

_____

_____

_____

_____

_____

_____

_____

I wish...

Use the 'I wish' to give yourself a chance to imagine a 'redo' or to think about how things might be different. Then take that thought and make a change, or act on it, if possible. For instance, "I wish I could be more open with my wife about my real feelings."

Sometimes writing it can help you say it out loud or act on it in another way. What do you wish?

I wish _____

_____

_____

_____

I wish _____

_____

_____

_____

I wish _____

_____

_____

_____

Resources

A Guide For Fathers When a Baby Dies, Tim Nelson, 2004, revised 2007, www.APlacetoRemember.com.

Empty Arms: Coping with Miscarriage, Stillbirth, and Infant Death...Surviving the First Hours and Beyond, Sherokee Ilse, 1982, revised 2008, www.WintergreenPress.com.

For Better or Worse, For Couples Whose Child has Died, Maribeth Wilder Doerr, 1992.

From Sorrow to Serenity, Susan Fletcher, 1998, Hunter House Publications.

Miscarriage: A Man's Book, Rick Wheat, 1995, Centering Corporation.

Healing Together: For Couples Grieving the Death of Their Baby, Marcie Lister and Sandra Lovell, 1991, revised 2004, Centering Corporation.

Help Your Marriage Survive The Death of a Child, Paul Rosenblatt, 2000, Temple University Press.

Men and Grief: A Guide for Men Surviving the Death of a Loved One, Carol Staudacher, 1991, New Harbinger Publications.

Men are from Mars, Women from Venus, John Gray, 1993, revised 2004.

Men Don't Cry, Women Do, T.L. Martin, K.J. Doka, 1999, Brunner.

Miscarriage: Women Sharing from the Heart, Marie Alen, Shelly Marks, 1993, Wiley Press.

Strong and Tender, Pat Schweiber, RN, Perinatal Loss, 1996 and 2003, www.griefwatch.com.

We Lost Our Baby: One Couple's Story of Miscarriage and its Aftermath, Siobhan O'Neill-White and David White, 2007 Liffey Press, www.the liffeypress.com.

A Place To Remember, 1885 University Ave. W., Ste 110, St. Paul, MN 55104; 800-631-0973; FAX 651-645-4780; www.APlaceToRemember.com

Wintergreen Press, Inc., 3630 Eileen St., Maple Plain, MN 55359; 952-476-1303; www.wintergreenpress.com